David M. Brennan
Financial Advisor

14785 Preston Rd., Ste. 780
Dallas, TX 75254
Ph: 972.980.PLAN
800.626.PLAN
Fax: 972.980.7859

BRENNAN
FINANCIAL SERVICES

Wishing Won't Do It

Wishing Won't Do It
Financial Planning Will

DAVE BRENNAN

BROWN BOOKS
PUBLISHING GROUP

Wishing Won't Do It
Financial Planning Will
© 2008 Dave Brennan

Manufactured in the United States of America

For information, please contact:

Brown Books Publishing Group
16200 North Dallas Parkway, Suite 170
Dallas, Texas 75248
www.brownbooks.com
972-381-0009

A New Era in Publishing™

ISBN-13: 978-1-934812-11-2
ISBN-10: 1-934812-11-0
LCCN: 2008926898

1 2 3 4 5 6 7 8 9 10

Dedication

THIS BOOK IS DEDICATED TO MY WONDERFUL FAMILY.

My wife Sandy knows how to lovingly point out the way to do things. You are the wind beneath my wings.

All four of our children have surprised me in their approach to life. Each one has a very strong tendency to make things happen. Michelle, David, Darren, and Debra I am so glad you joined me on my journey through life.

My lifelong gratitude to the many educators, particularly the nuns, Christian brothers, and Jesuits who taught me what a good life is about.

To the country I love for providing all of the incredible opportunities that allowed me to succeed. Now it is my chance to give back.

Acknowledgments

This is my first book, so I needed lots of hand holding to understand the progression and timetable through the publishing process.

From the moment I met Milli Brown, of Brown Books Publishing Group, and saw the high level of interest she showed for the book, I felt confident that a success story was in the making.

Kathryn Grant was always very clear and correct with her English lessons; Janet Harris, PhD, brought her organizational skills for clarity; Latham Shinder shared his expertise for structuring thoughts and positioning ideas; Bill Young's creative illustrations and book design reinforced the concepts of the text; and Cindy Birne's and Cathy Williams' energy and expertise have book marketing and PR down to a science.

They all get a big thanks for their personal commitment and expertise that I absolutely needed to make this happen.

TABLE OF CONTENTS

Introduction
Wishing Won't Do It

The lethargy and decadence that characterized the fall of the Roman Empire should have influenced the way the rest of the world behaves. It didn't. Why have so many nations since the Romans experienced the same fatal mistakes by becoming fat, dumb, and happy? Subsequent nations had vast resources yet somehow wasted those resources in shameful ways, and it's still going on.

The kind of waste I'm referring to isn't happening just in other countries. This kind of waste is happening right here at home. In the last thirty years, many Americans have stopped thinking about the common good and instead turned inward and become habitually self-centered.

Consider how many are entertainment junkies, addicted to twenty-four-hour satellite television, movie rentals, talk radio, late-night infomercials. We're obsessive about getting hold of the latest electronic gadget, and we buy bigger and bigger vehicles. We pay for most of these goodies on credit and in the process destroy the family budget. Instant gratification has become the American norm. If this trend continues to grow, the collapse of our economy and our American way of life is not an unreasonable expectation.

Well, I don't want to see that happen. One of the reasons I wrote this book is to make all of us aware of how destructive instant gratification can be. I want to see our country filled with ever-expanding opportunities for our children and grandchildren. Subsequent generations should experience the same level of excitement that filled our souls when we were kids. I want them to lead hopeful lives centered on a loving family that is financially secure and protected by a fiscally sound federal government.

Today, restaurants have largely replaced the kitchen table where families traditionally enjoyed private conversations about daily activities. What ever happened to family members sharing their personal achievements, big and small? The very notion of family bonding is disappearing. Divorces are tearing apart the fiber of our culture. On the national level, the federal debt is completely out of control. Taken as a whole, these changes are all very bad for the future of America.

With respect to retirement, what are your plans for the time when you're no longer employed? While most Americans desperately want to retire in comfort, many haven't saved enough money for the big event. How, then, can you have any hope of achieving the American dream of financial security? That would be a horrible ending to such a wonderful journey of life!

This book is all about money and how we treat it. When we don't respect it, we spend most of our lives wishing for things we may never get. Have you ever had these thoughts?

- I wish we could afford a nice vacation.

- I wish I had more money to buy things.

- I wish we were out of debt.

- I wish we had a nicer home.

- I wish we had a better car.

- I wish I had new clothes.

- I wish I could afford health insurance.

- I wish our politicians were honest and responsible about our budget.

- I wish our country was out of this horrible debt.

- I wish we would be comfortable in retirement.

- I wish I could afford to send my children to college.

How many times have you found yourself wishing for any of these items? My question to you is will those wishes ever be fulfilled? Wishing can go on and on, but eventually we learn that wishing won't do it; family financial planning will.

By family financial planning, I'm referring to a complete set of economic values regarding money. Your personal future depends on your financial habits and the changes necessary to help you make better financial decisions going forward. This book addresses ways to make those changes, how to think about money, and what exactly to do with it after you earn it.

By reading this book, you will learn the important difference between savings and investments. I have included comments about the benefits of tax-free and tax-deferred programs to help you reduce taxes while you build your retirement nest egg. To be financially successful, you and the rest of your family must be committed to improving your financial habits.

With respect to credit card debt, you will find ways to eliminate the debt and then stay out of debt. I offer helpful ideas for your family, and I've included a section on the important "Rule of 72," which helps savers and investors understand how quickly money doubles. This information can help in deciding which saving or investment program to consider for long-term growth.

The Opportunities Are Out There

When you think of the history of America, much of our growth came from entrepreneurs who created jobs through business opportunities. Stories abound about rags-to-riches families who started with nothing and became wildly successful. I happen to be one of those stories.

Born of Irish immigrants, I have two parents who came from large families raised in two-bedroom houses without water, plumbing, or electricity. Their education was in the school of hard knocks. I was the first in the family to get a college degree. My education required eight years at night, and I did it while I was married, raising a family, and traveling with my job. On top of that, I had a second job on the weekends that allowed us to pay cash for all our purchases—a strategy that worked wonders for my family and will very likely work for yours. One year our finances were so tight that we had to make a choice between putting retread tires on our only car or taking a vacation. So what did we do? We put the retreads on the car and rode on a bus to Ocean City, New Jersey, for a one-day vacation.

As you read this book, don't limit your possible success with thoughts of *If only . . . or Yes, but. . . .* I know how hard it is to have limited financial means. But I made a decision to turn my limited opportunities into a journey of success. You can too. Open your mind to financial security and you can change your life forever.

I

Life
Strategies

"Our financial plan is working."

1

Success Comes from Good Habits

> Every person born into the world represents something new and exciting that never existed before. Life should be treated as a great journey, because it is.

In the neighborhood where I grew up, in Llanerch Hills outside of Philadelphia, Pennsylvania, many of the workers were union members with their income and career paths pretty much set in stone once they chose their trades. At an early age, these men knew their station in life, because workers' hourly salary was published in the city paper. The only way to earn more was by working harder and getting overtime pay. Something inside me said "no" to that system.

In my late teens, we all gathered in the evenings at a neighborhood bar to tell stories, play darts and other games, and drink a couple of brews. After two years of this activity, and with all the well-worn stories growing bigger than life, I became bored. One summer night I said to the fellows that this was my last time in the bar, and I left. I stopped drinking beer and never returned.

My leaving the bar wasn't an important event for my friends, but it was monumental for me. I enrolled in night school and spent eight years, winter and summer, at St Joseph's University in Philadelphia to earn a degree in business and philosophy. Why eight years? I had slow teachers. That's my story, and I'm sticking to it.

One night in class, we discussed how many mediocre students like me became leaders of corporations or started their own successful businesses. Until then, I believed that since I came from a family with no college education and very low income, I also was predestined for the same economic level of achievement. I thought wealthy parents produced wealthy kids and poor parents produced poor kids. Fortunately, in this great country, that's not the way it has to be.

As we discussed career opportunities in our marketing courses, for the first time in my life I was flooded with excitement for my future. When we went around the room for comments, the students were asked to talk about their business dreams. I said I wanted to start my own company. But unlike the rest of the students, who said big income was their goal, I wanted my company to do wonderful things for others while building a better country.

I've always had a strong feeling of pride as an American. As a guy in his early twenties, I didn't know what direction to pursue, but somehow, I was sure I could succeed. I had a fire burning in my gut that encouraged me to look for better ways to do things. In fact, on several occasions my wife asked me if I was trying to change the world. I thought that someday, yes, I might be able to change part of it.

For me, a college education was a wonderful breakthrough. Upon graduation, I was recruited by a new employer, received a sizeable increase in pay, and never looked back. After twenty-five years in the petroleum industry, I organized my own investment firm and started in the direction of my dream.

For centuries, most countries maintained a class system that controlled the economic status of each family. In America, the only limitations are those we put in our own minds. By forming good habits and changing our approach to money matters, we can all experience financial success.

Follow Your Dreams, but First Wake Up

Many friends, family members, and co-workers thought I was suffering from a mid-life crisis when I told them of my plan to leave a large corporation to start my firm. I constantly heard, "What, and give up all the benefits? You're crazy and selfish!" They all wanted to know what my wife Sandy thought about this silly idea. When I told them she wanted me to quit right away, they were mystified.

I've come to realize that only our dreams of a better life can lift us from a negative station. A strong belief in a greater tomorrow can motivate us to reach a higher level. The changes may not be easy, but there is no courage without fear. Starting a business with nothing behind me but sheer determination for success was a challenge that I will never forget.

When It Starts

Early childhood is all about immediate choices. If a child does something good, mom and dad clap their hands and praise loudly. Parental approval is an immediate reward for good behavior. However, if a child chooses bad behavior, he receives no positive reinforcement. Each of us learned early on what would please family and friends.

Kindergarten and grade school presented another reward system to help us distinguish good performance from bad. The reward might have been a gold star on our paper, less homework that night, or perhaps the applause of the class for our special achievement. The process worked well because we knew immediately the result of our choices and our actions.

But once we went to work, we discovered the reward system was dramatically different. When we demonstrated business skills that contributed to the growth of the company, our salaries were increased and benefits expanded. Then we were offered participation in a self-managed 401(k), 403(b), or 457 retirement plan. And that's where the reward system suddenly hit a wall. What did we know about investing? For the first time in our lives, we had to make important decisions on our own about the company plan's investment choices, and these decisions would directly affect our retirement income. Worse, we had no immediate reward system to measure the success of our choices. We were told of the investment's past performance and, in the same breath, told that past performance was no indication of future results.

What exactly does this disclosure really mean, and why is it printed on all investment literature? We all know that most things don't perform as well as they did when they were brand new. We're big kids; we know that light bulbs blow out, refrigerators stop working, furniture wears out, TVs break, air conditioners need to be replaced, and our computers with all their wizardry sometimes lock up and won't perform.

But there is no other warning like the one on our invest-ment information. This warning is like a sign telling us to avoid the investments that have performed so well for years and years. Unfortunately, that fearsome warning has become a major reason millions of workers do not participate in employer-sponsored programs. The warning has simply scared them off focusing only on the potential negative losses and not on the potential benefits of long-term investing.

Choose to Be Positive

If you want to be treated differently, you have to act differ-ently. During our lifetime, certain people influence each of us in negative ways, but you can choose to be positive. In many family circles, a strong dominant member prematurely estab-lishes an expectation for everyone else in the family. If someone in your family has positioned you at the bottom of the family totem pole, it's time to quietly decline the position.

The first thing you do is minimize the amount of time spent with that person. Why? Because you've decided to become a better person, one who wants to be financially secure and not dependent on your friends or family for your success. This single action can generate a great feeling of confidence.

Avoid Unnecessary Distractions

From the mid 1980s forward, most Americans have become distracted with the ever-expanding range of new technology, from laptops and cell phones, to GPS in our cars and break-through video gaming systems. We've become followers of the latest fads, and we want immediate results, also known as "instant gratification." Unfortunately, in the same way, we expect our investments to provide instant performance. This has created a severe negative effect in the way we relate to money. Consider how much time and effort we devote to learning all the features of our latest cell phone versus how little time we devote to learning about investment vehicles.

Be Yourself

Choice is an important part of the freedom we enjoy in America. The freedom to choose allows us to make daily decisions that can help us achieve success. Our choices have nothing to do with where we were born, our heritage, or our family. We can't change our past, but we can change our future, and it's the future where you will spend the rest of your life.

When I was young, I heard family members talk about the day "their ship would come in." After a while, I started responding, "Hey, if it doesn't come in, why not swim out and climb aboard?" We can always change our outlook for the future. One way is by pursuing useful information. Another is by staying positive in the face of adversity. Remaining positive can move us forward emotionally, physically, and financially, even while others around us are paralyzed with indecision and excuses for not being successful.

The next time you feel uncertain about a financial decision, imagine you are part of a team, and all around you, team members are waving their arms and giving you high fives (or the hand claps from our childhood). Think of the wonderful results you can achieve through taking financial control of your life.

How to Use Your Money Responsibly

Here is a really wacky problem that needs to be addressed. I know sports is a big thing in our country, but I'm constantly amazed to hear about low income families that spend thousands each year for season tickets to NBA, NFL, or NHL games. These families spend money on parking, beer, hot dogs, and souvenirs and later complain they don't have any money to invest in their company 401(k). The question is, *why?* These people have made enormously poor choices.

Consider the family that has several credit cards (many families admit to having twelve or more) and is making only minimum monthly payments. The monthly debt becomes overwhelming, yet they continue to purchase new products and services on credit. These folks have no self control, and many appeal to other family members to bail them out.

The obvious solution to credit card debt is to begin making good financial choices. Pay off credit card debt and avoid impulse buying. Plan your purchases before you go out to buy anything, and implement the simplest and most powerful tool: set priorities for your financial goals. Buying the latest toys for your children and yourself is far less important than buying food in retirement, isn't it?

Financial Security Is Not Male or Female

My wife and I have four adult children close in age, two boys and two girls. When our boys were young, I noticed a ritual when they had their friends in the house. They couldn't walk by each other without a friendly bump or poke in the stomach. Boys have a strong tendency to make physical contact at a young age, as though they are training for future combat. As I watched the boys' behavior, I decided to try a similar exercise with my girls. Playfully, I bumped into my girls in a mild game of shoulder pushing. The idea was to toughen them up. My wife Sandy thought I'd left my senses, but now, years later, the girls tell us it was a great source of fun. They liked it because of the attention they received and at the same time learned to compete in a playful way both emotionally and physically.

Fifty years ago I envisioned a change that would sweep across America to place women and their talents right in the center of career growth. Fortunately, I was right. This change was a new and powerful paradigm that helps to level the playing field for women who have the skills and are prepared to accept new responsibilities. What a wonderful change! Our two daughters fit that description perfectly. They are wives and mothers, and each has built a large investment practice in Dallas, Texas.

Teach Your Children to Speak Confidently

To improve our children's opportunities, we started a weekly speaking program in our home, which included all family members. The program originally began with a one-minute presentation on a subject selected by each speaker. Every week I was the first to start the presentations to help get everyone settled down to a workable routine. Each speaker stood in front of a large fireplace in our family room. The speeches were somewhat awkward in the beginning, as the kids watched each other develop their own speaking skills. After several months of weekly exercises, and as the speeches were expanded to five minutes, it was difficult to get them to sit down. The genie was out of the bottle. From that point on, a new level of confidence was evident during spirited family conversations.

Think of the highly gifted individuals who could contribute to the world, but can't communicate properly. Developing speaking skills should be a mandatory course in every year of school. Public speaking encourages each child to use better diction while bringing mountains of confidence to underperformers. Shyness should be only a word for the dictionary. Now think of your children speaking confidently about their financial security and what they did to achieve the success they are experiencing.

Be Positive

Each day we are becoming who we will be tomorrow. Some of us grow in positive ways because we are surrounded by supportive families and friends. Perhaps you and I are fortunate to have earned a college degree. If we are lucky, we choose a lucrative career.

Not everyone is so fortunate. Many people feel separated from the successful part of society and in this separation grow each day in negative ways. These individuals often turn to frightening behavior to escape their feelings of failure. As an extreme example, school shootings have shocked the nation. What a loss for this one-time journey called life! Everyone has some person or some event to blame for not being successful. But a constant focus on the many positive opportunities can help you improve your life forever.

Create Change with Your Actions

America is a society that likes entertainment. When celebrities or public figures do good or bad, the effects can be widespread. For example, I marvel at Oprah Winfrey, who wisely designed her show to help millions see the opportunity for a better life. Think of all the positive reinforcement she continuously brings her viewers. She encourages her audience to consider the good qualities of her guests. My wife Sandy constantly tells me who Oprah had on her programs that day and what a wonderful message she brought to her audience.

However, we don't have to be on TV to make a positive influence on others. Each of us can be an agent of change in our family, workplace, or community. I challenge you to be that positive person in your circle of influence.

CHOOSE TO SLOW DOWN

In the 1980s, most Americans began moving at incredible speeds. Speed limits were increased, our cars and SUVs got bigger, communication technology improved, and our lives got busier. In the 1990s, this pace increased to such a degree that family therapists talked of distracted parents scheduling employee sick days to catch up on activities like getting in touch with their children or paying bills. We all know some parents who spend much of their weekends driving from one sporting event to another so their children can participate in as many events as possible. These are time-challenged parents who brag about accomplishing so much yet constantly look frazzled and worn out.

Don't be one of these parents. Consider devoting the same amount of time to your children, but in quieter moments, functioning as moms and dads. Spend these times talking about family backgrounds or cultural interests. Turn off your phone. Get face to face with your child. Listen.

ARE YOU CONTROLLED?

As soon as the technology became available, many employers wanted to stay in touch with their employees 24/7 and did so by issuing company pagers. Then cell phones arrived, accompanied by tiny headsets and wireless earpieces. Regardless of the approach, corporate communications infringed on our family time capturing employees' attention every minute of every day. Our private lives have become compromised for the sake of positioning ourselves for a promotion or continued job security.

As cell phone reception improved, it seemed as if everybody felt compelled to have a phone in hand. In many circles, these devices became status symbols. For some, they were proudly displayed as badges of distinction. And each tiny cell phone came with a loud ring, as if these sounds were meant to convey importance. Worst of all, many cell phone users thought their conversations had to be continued anywhere, any time, and under any circumstances, on a non-stop basis. Good grief!

Public rudeness resulting from cell phone use has taken on another dimension. I often hear passengers waiting to board planes, trains, buses, and automobiles, talking loudly on their cells about business and personal activities, dinner plans, movies, weather, finances, sexual experiences, and world events. And all this is carried on while disregarding others in the immediate area. A cell phone held to the ear seems to give many the illusion that they can talk—sometimes holler— above others, as though their phone call was the world's most important event at that moment. It's not.

The phone companies tell us that most cell phones are purchased through credit cards. For some plans, the higher the use, the higher the cost, but most users don't realize the expense because it goes on the credit card. When is the last time you heard any of your friends say they are going to cut back on cell phone use because of the cost? With the introduction of text messaging, I can almost imagine my grandkids with callused thumbs that have outgrown their fingers.

And here is the scary part: many drivers are observed talking on a phone as they weave in and out of traffic at high speeds. The enormous downside to all this is the mounting pressure to watch out for distracted drivers, adding another layer of stress to our lives. Studies have shown that a distracted driver is more dangerous than a drunk driver.

We are running faster and faster without devoting enough quiet time to planning for our financial future. It's time to slow down, be courteous, and pay more attention to your financial goals. Retirement may seem like a long way off, but so did turning 50.

TO-DO LIST OF
LIFE

☑ Graduate from college
☑ Start career
☑ Pay off student loan
☑ Buy car
☑ Get married
☑ Purchase home
☑ Start family
☐ Invest for education
☐ Invest for retirement

"Gosh, I have so many things to do."

2

Life Is What Happens While You Are Doing Other Things

The search for quality in life
has no limits.

In 1990, in the middle of one of my financial seminars, a woman sitting in the front row abruptly stood up. She introduced herself as Mary and said she was in her fifties and this was her first financial seminar. Mary told the group, "Getting old is difficult, but getting old without money is hell." She paused for a moment and then said, "I should have attended this seminar fifteen years ago."

As suddenly as she stood, she sat back in her chair. The room remained eerily quiet. I never forgot her comments—not for what she said, but for what she didn't say that everyone in the room somehow seemed to hear. She believed that it was too late to improve her financial life—too late for financial planning to have any significant impact. There had been too much spending and very little saving. When Mary became a client, we talked about her seminar experience. She told me that the comments were not just about herself, but also about her friends and family who were now struggling in retirement with no realistic hope of improving their lives.

It's never too late to achieve financial security. You can do it, and *Wishing Won't Do It* can help you get there.

SMART MONEY DEFINED

Acting smart with your money requires applying simple but powerful concepts. They will keep you focused on being family financial planners and investors. This book is intended for use by millions of Americans who find financial matters intimidating, confusing, overwhelming, frightening, or just plain boring. If you follow the strategies outlined in this book, you will have an opportunity to reach your financial goals, build family wealth for generations to come, and improve the financial health of our great country. That's a big claim, I know, but one I fully believe is achievable.

Wishing Won't Do It is more than a list of money management techniques. It describes a philosophy about our relationship to money, family, career, aging, governance, and taxes. It includes ideas about our overall personal, community, and national financial stability; also it explores some of the root causes that weaken the financial wellness of individuals, neighborhoods, and the nation. These causes range from too much debt and lack of family financial planning to the waste of family resources through bad habits. The book's philosophy centers on the basic relationship between a sound mind and healthy body, supported by the application of working assets.

WORKING ASSETS—THE INCOME GENERATORS

Most Americans have not understood the importance of investing their hard-earned money in the right investments. The right investments typically have two goals—growth and income. Financial investing is misunderstood because it's not taught at home or in school. Here is Primer One.

Working assets are the ones that generate income. They are very important because they are the foundation of security in your family financial plan. When you learn this concept, you will intuitively seek the highest rate of return, within the shortest period of time, at the highest level of safety.

Smart investors focus on all three parts of the equation: return, time, and safety. Many untrained in the investment field focus only on safety, because their biggest concern is losing their money. Nobody wants to lose money. But here is the problem with that narrow kind of thinking: by focusing on a single variable, you miss the biggest advantage investing has to offer, which is long-term growth.

So now you know that working assets are the income generators that produce dependable monthly cash flow. This cash flow will define your lifestyle in retirement. What you have to learn further is the types of working assets that fit your risk/reward profile. Reread this section to plant the information firmly in your mind. As you evaluate your investment portfolio, consider these three key variables—return, time, and safety—for each investment in your portfolio.

ARE YOU STARTING TO FEEL THE EXCITEMENT?

This book is not an academic exercise or scholastic workout to prove a vague theoretical point. Rather, it's intended to help you realize, perhaps for the first time, that regardless of background, education, or income, you can achieve financial security through sound family financial planning. One great advantage of our country is that opportunities for learning never stop. You might be surprised to learn about the many millionaires and billionaires who never set foot on a college campus. Whatever your age or formal education, here is your chance to learn a system to reach higher levels of financial success.

The strategies described in this book are based on six decades of experience as an American, husband, father, and advisor in the financial services industry. This experience includes twenty-three years on my weekly radio and TV call-in programs helping listeners make complex financial decisions. I have written this book to help people like you achieve your dream of financial security.

For most Americans, financial security should mean having money in working assets while minimizing or eliminating debt. Yet many haven't accomplished either objective. Why? I believe people lack the knowledge about simple, achievable strategies like those described in the next several chapters. And, of course, many people have formed bad financial habits over the years, which compound the problems of investing for retirement.

The Start of Brennan Financial Services

I worked in the petroleum industry for twenty-five years before leaving Mobil Oil Corporation in 1984. I joined the company in Philadelphia and later transferred to Los Angeles and then to Dallas. Part of my responsibilities as a tax manager was to travel the country and to evaluate the company's assets for local property tax purposes.

In the mid-1970s, I became disappointed with the way Mobil's senior management was allocating company capital for non-energy projects. In particular, when Mobil announced the purchase of the department store chain Montgomery Ward, I nearly fell out of my chair.

As a regional tax manager, I routinely traveled to appraise the value of company assets for property tax purposes. During these many trips, I observed that Montgomery Ward was out of touch with its customers and steadily losing sales and profits. Founded as the world's first mail order business in 1872, Montgomery Ward was, at its height, one of the largest retailers in the United States. By the 1970s, the company couldn't keep pace with its rivals: Sears, JCPenney, Macy's, and Dillard's. And yet here was Mobil, flush with cash, trying to convince the employees and shareholders that spending billions on a sinking ship was a solid investment.

The only Mobil personnel who benefited from the acquisition were the top brass, many of whom received sizeable salary increases and more stock options. The company had definitely changed, and not in a good way. In 1988, Mobil sold its interest in Montgomery Ward, while openly admitting the expensive acquisition and subsequent redesign of store layouts into boutique-like specialty stores was a complete failure. As an employee and stockholder, I witnessed this sad chain of events first hand.

But the big issue for me was that I slowly lost interest in what I had always thought of as *my* company.

In 1982, I got serious about a career in financial planning. I developed a relationship with a financial services firm in Dallas. Each evening after work for two years, I joined the firm to discuss client investments, tax strategies, and computer applications for gathering information. My initial focus was consulting for defined-benefit pension plans for medical practitioners. For months, I researched investment strategies and related tax considerations. Although the clientele was primarily in the medical services industry, high net worth entrepreneurs and corporate executives were also attracted to the projected financial and tax benefits and soon became clients.

I wanted a new challenge in a different direction and immediately realized that providing personal financial services was it. In early 1983, while still employed at Mobil, I sat for several securities exams required by the industry. That same year, I took on a large group of clients all working for the same corporation. These employees lived in major cities across the country. Each had substantial stock options and, because the company was restructuring for a potential spin-off, the options had to be exercised in a timely fashion to achieve the special benefits. Do it right, and you could parlay the options into a healthy retirement plan. Do it wrong, and you could end up with complicated tax problems for years.

On weekends, I traveled to various offices and homes across the country to explain investment and tax strategies to each participant. The effort was extremely successful, and soon I had built a thriving referral business. Before long I had more clients outside of Texas than I had in the state.

To attract local clients, I started presenting weekly financial planning seminars in libraries, hotels, and corporate offices in the Dallas/Ft. Worth area. As my practice continued to grow, I resigned my position with Mobil in 1984 and opened Brennan Financial Services. Gradually my four children joined the firm, and today we are recognized as a family business.

When asked if I have any reservations about my decision to leave the security of a company like Mobil, or about my career choices, I say, "Sure, I wish I'd gotten into personal financial planning sooner." Of course, the decision was very risky at the time, but in life only those who take on risk should be rewarded. I love what I do because it's not a job; it's a career.

The Company Will Take Care of Me, Right?

During my long career with Mobil, I routinely heard a mantra that goes something like this: "No matter what happens, the company will take care of us." The big problem with that belief is that it isn't true. Times have changed dramatically in most corporations, and yet the vast majority of employees in the 1970s, '80s, and even the '90s looked upon their employers as something akin to a benevolent parent.

Many employees who work for large corporations still believe the company will take care of them right through retirement. Only a strange thread of luck will see that dream come true. Why? Because many workers will be employed by eight to ten different employers in a lifetime, with each company having its own program of employee benefits—401(k)s, stock options, bonuses, lifetime annuities, stock purchase plans, college savings plans, health insurance, and other offerings. Managing so many financial decisions during the transition from one job to the next can be a frightening experience, even for experts. Further, retirement planning and management can be downright overwhelming for a novice. That's why top executives have advisors help them sort out the benefit plans.

It's interesting that many large corporations provide personal financial planning to the executive group as a company benefit, but employees below that rank—because they are recognized as experts in their own fields—wouldn't think of hiring an advisor on their own, although they certainly need one. I wonder how they would react if they found out the top dogs are getting free company-sponsored advice.

The next time you look for a position with a new company, here's some of the best advice you could get. During the job interview, ask what type of pension plan is available for your position. Here again, top executives usually are offered several added incentives in their compensation package. If a retirement plan is not immediately available for you, ask how soon you will be eligible for one. If none is offered, consider another employer. If that's not an option, contact your financial advisor to seek information about setting up a monthly systematic investment program in your own IRA or Roth IRA or a private pension in an annuity. There are hundreds of personal investment plans that will fit your risk/reward profile.

If you are self-employed, you had better know how to take care of your retirement benefits. The sky is the limit with defined contribution and defined benefit plans and your investment opportunities are more extensive than in a corporation. Ask your advisor to review how your compensation is structured to develop a pension plan unique to your company.

"Financial security requires
planning ahead."

3

Financial Security
Means Different Things

As you consider your financial
security, have you noticed that the
future keeps getting closer and closer?

Many in the financial services industry refer to financial security as "financial independence" or "financial freedom." These are all acceptable terms, but I personally prefer "financial security" because it's the term my female clients use most often. In meetings with clients, I often ask, "What does having enough money mean to you?" To men, having enough can mean lots of things. To most women, money means just one thing: financial security.

How much is enough and how financially secure you'll be in retirement are up to you. For purposes of this book, think of financial security in terms of having enough working assets—money in a savings account, stocks, bonds, real estate, pension plans, mutual fund, annuities, IRAs, ownership in businesses, and any other income generators that can be used during retirement—to maintain your lifestyle. Retirement is that period in life when you can stop working for money and your money works for you.

What Are Your Goals?

So what is your working asset target number? Is it five hundred thousand, a million, ten million, or a whopping one hundred million? You choose because it's your life and your number. There are no limits! We all have the same sky, but not the same horizons.

Next, consider what date you will retire.

From a family planning perspective, these two numbers aren't as important as having a committed family making every effort to get there. This book can be the basic teaching tool for your personal plan. When I began presenting financial planning seminars in the early 1980s, some attendees questioned some of my positive math comments. I routinely said that if you invested a certain amount each month with a precise rate of return for forty years, you would accumulate $1,000,000 for retirement.

Some attendees questioned the rationale of monthly investing. Others wondered what a million would be worth in twenty years. I have always responded in the same way: "A million dollars will be worth a million dollars, and that's a lot more than you'll have, if you do nothing." The idea was all about starting to invest now to accumulate whatever amount is possible for retirement income. Why challenge a successful strategy?

Achievers in Life Are Those Who Respond the Best and Quickest to Change

To change your life, remove the self-imposed limits that have prevented you from creating family wealth. We know that financial security is the ability to maintain your lifestyle without working. Financial security means having enough working assets generating monthly income to pay your bills and provide the lifestyle of your dreams. Financial security also means having a comfortable retirement for the rest of your life, but it doesn't necessarily mean retirement now. Many of you can achieve financial security at an early age and continue to enjoy your careers.

Nothing is so habit forming as money that includes both good and bad habits. Most Americans know how to make money, but don't know what to do with it once they have it. Why? Because money comes to us without instructions. Our education system fails to offer even basic training in money management. Think back—in what class did you learn how to balance your checkbook? Where was that elusive class Money 101 when we needed it?

To make matters worse, the subject's terms, formulas, and complicated financial instruments can be overwhelming. This confusion is so widespread that millions of ordinary savers and investors quietly suffer deep frustration and fear every year. They think they're the only ones in the country who can't understand financial terms and their proper applications. This frustration renders them helpless and prevents many families from taking advantage of the potential profits that others have enjoyed for decades. Collectively, most Americans are doing poorly with respect to investing because they've never understood what to do with their money to ensure a comfortable retirement in the future. Hopefully this book will serve as a useful primer to help families build wealth, reduce debt, and change the way they think about money.

The Two Parts of Money

Money has two equally important and powerful parts—buying power and psychological power. *Buying power* is the ability to purchase goods and services when you need them. Generally, the more money we make, the more we spend. This is easy enough to understand, but something else is going on here. The more we earn, the higher our expectations for quality in the things we buy. As our overall standard of living increases, we look for better food, shelter, clothing, education, and medical treatment and other services. Because they cost more, we can get caught up in a spiral where all our income is spent maintaining our higher standard of living and fail to establish dedicated investment accounts for the future.

The *psychological power* of money refers to how it makes us feel. Money inspires confidence. Money makes us feel safe. Money can turn negative emotions into positive ones. The lack of money, on the other hand, can leave us at the mercy of the world around us. Without money, we may lose our dignity and self-esteem. But we shouldn't feel that way. You can change your life if you really want to. Combining the two parts of money—buying power and psychological power—can produce extraordinary results in your life.

These forces can also oppose each other. In many households, each spouse has a different economic or emotional attraction to money—what it means and, more profoundly, what it represents with respect to spending and saving. When these forces are substantially out of sync, the results can be disastrous to the entire family. Remember, the number one reason for divorce is differences over money.

Consider a spouse obsessed with liquidating assets to pay off the mortgage, while the other spouse wants to keep the money working in investments. We know that taking a large amount from investments to pay off a mortgage will permanently reduce the earning power of that money to zero. The investment-oriented spouse points out that, if the assets continued working, earning 6% to10% per year, there would be more income to make the monthly mortgage payments. Also, in the event of an emergency, that spouse contends, it's easier to access the money. On the other hand, withdrawing income from "bricks and mortar" can be difficult.

The reality is that many Americans "buy up" after the current mortgage is paid off. They continue to take money that should be directed to investments to pay off the house and then use the equity to buy a bigger house. The result is a bigger home and fewer working assets to produce income in retirement.

To help settle this ongoing debate, here is a simple formula to help you decide whether to pay off the mortgage or keep the money in a tax-deferred account: Multiply your mortgage rate by one minus your federal income tax rate. For example with a mortgage rate of 6% and a 35% tax rate, you would multiply 6% by 0.65 (1.00 − 0.35 = 0.65) to arrive at 3.9%. Can you get a better rate of return through a tax-deferred investment? The formula has to be applied differently if you have additional state income tax or if you are taking a standard deduction on your return. This provides the basis for an economic answer; however, "I sleep better at night" without a mortgage may be the final answer.

My point here is not whether to pay off your mortgage (one or both of you will eventually make the right decision for your family), but that any family financial plan is more powerful and effective if both spouses have the same goals and dreams for retirement. And this brings us back to the central question of this chapter: "What does financial security mean to you?" If you can't come up with an answer right away, now might be a good time for some serious thought.

As you think about your financial future, consider these important areas:

- Monthly income during retirement

- Financing higher education

- Owning your home without a mortgage

- Leaving a legacy for your family

A wonderful exercise here is to have each spouse rank the goals in terms of importance while considering the potential for each one being achieved.

"Will I ever get out of debt?"

4

Reduce Debt Each Month

> Consider the lesson of the pyramids.
> Each brick is insignificant, but
> collectively they represent one of the
> great wonders of the world.

Taxation is the process of the government taking dollars from each of us and distributing the money among the various governmental agencies until it disappears. Our current national tax and budgeting process is a terrible system.

As of July 2007, the U.S. federal debt had reached $8.8 trillion, which puts each taxpayer's share at roughly $30,000. If that isn't enough to shock you, our national spending is accelerating. Research analysts tell us that our national debt has increased an average of $1.3 billion *per day* since September 29, 2006. At this rate, we will soon reach the current federal debt limit of $9.0 trillion When that happens, Congress will have to raise the federal debt ceiling once again to increase the nation's credit limit, resulting in more devaluation of our dollar compared to other currencies. Just say $9 trillion several times to get the full effect of what the politicians in Washington are doing to our nation. Staggering, isn't it? No other country in the history of the world has wasted so much wealth as the United States. Not even the Romans.

When political economists discuss our national debt, they try desperately to convince us that spending at that level is fine for the economy. On the contrary, the growing federal debt should be an enormous source of embarrassment to the White House and Congress. Unfortunately, they seem oblivious to the problem.

In my opinion, elected officials in Washington are behaving irresponsibly by sinking our country deeper into debt without consideration for ever paying it down. Our increased national debt is particularly painful when so much is sent to foreign countries for political favors. Our politicians don't seem to understand that you can't buy friends; you can only rent them. The expanded bad habit of pork-barrel waste presents another questionable future for our children and grandchildren. And that's not right.

Incidentally, as each presidential election approaches, have you heard any of the candidates discuss this moral question of growing debt? Not one. In fact, the political platforms are about increased spending for health care insurance that will result in further debt for our country. Stop the nonsense. Stop it!

As you consider the debt of our country, don't you wonder about the economic reports from Washington advising us that employment is on the rise? That simply means more Americans are working, and more are paying taxes. Although we have the largest employment base ever generating more tax revenue to Washington, our national debt continues to grow. How can this be? How long can this continue before the system fails?

The reason for this problem is simple: the federal government continues to spend more than it receives in tax revenues.

This overspending mentality isn't restricted to liberals or conservatives, because our debt grows with each presidency. Both parties have demonstrated a keen ability to give billions away to get elected and billions more to be re-elected.

Off-budget items are now in the billions. Political pork-barrel legislation is at an all-time high. The term "pork-barrel legislation," for those who may not know, describes legislation that is loaded with special projects for members of Congress to distribute to their constituents back home as acts of largesse, courtesy of the federal taxpayer. Pork-barrel legislation is an ancient and despicable practice that needs to stop.

The saddest part of this whole story is the interest taxpayers are forced to absorb to service the enormous national debt. The national debt adds hundreds of billions each year, forever wasting tax dollars.

What has changed over the last thirty-five years is a focus on short-term gratification over long-term national achievements. We live in a country filled with politicians who care more about their legacy than the proper management of the annual budget. I love this country, but like a growing number of Americans, I'm fed up with what I see as blatant fiscal irresponsibility. Political expediency is in, and fiscal responsibility is out.

No country is willing to challenge America in a military conflict. But economically, many countries are taking us apart, piece by piece. America has now become a debtor nation that depends on other countries to buy our debt instruments on a regular basis, which results in a substantial loss in value of the American dollar. If you have traveled to the United Kingdom or Europe recently, you've witnessed firsthand the loss in value of the American dollar. Currently, the oil-producing countries are promoting the use of the Euro, the official currency of the Eurozone, over the U.S. dollar. If that happens, the American dollar will continue to weaken—a sign that the overall health of the American economy is struggling.

How about Your Personal Debt

In May 2007, the Federal Reserve announced that credit card debt had reached $872 billion, or about $9,200 per family. Credit card debt is expected to reach the unbelievable level of $15,000 per family within the next five to ten years. Much of this debt is the result of frivolous purchases, including entertainment, name brands bought just for the image, paying others to do work we could do, and impulse buying of the latest toy. Surveys tell us that credit card use is considered a primary way to accumulate frequent flyer miles, even though most airlines have substantially reduced the number of seats available for that purpose.

The problem with credit card debt is that many families can't make the required payments, and unlike our big spenders in Washington, are unable to raise their credit limit by printing more money. The number of Americans filing for bankruptcy jumped 30% in 2005, to the highest level on record. The extent of this problem is mind boggling, with more than two million individuals seeking bankruptcy protection that year. Equally discouraging is that they do so without recognizing their own responsibility, without understanding the mistakes they've made to reach this point, and without realizing that these same bad habits will result in more serious problems later in life. They seem to make no cause and effect connection between buying everything now and the balance on their monthly credit card statement.

In financial terms, there are two types of people: spenders and savers. The spenders look the other way when the monthly bills arrive in the mail. They spend more than they make, with credit card debt taking up the resulting shortfall. And credit card buying is expensive. You pay an enormous price for convenience.

Why is the credit card debt such a growing problem? Because many Americans make only minimum monthly payments. Then interest on the unpaid balance, together with late fees and other charges, substantially increases the borrower's debt. Late fees and underpayment fees can also be problems, ranging from $25 to $50 per customer each month. The total of these fees represents nearly a third of credit card company revenues. When you add on interest charges at 18% to 20% per year, the actual cost of each purchase increases significantly. A coat costing $100 purchased on a credit card without payments for a year cost $120 at 20% interest and $144 if unpaid after two years.

For some, credit card use has become addictive. Just think of the workout credit cards get during the Christmas shopping season. Most of us are familiar with friends and family members who promise to pay off Christmas shopping debt by June, but somehow never do. Why? Because January to June is a long time, and the folks with the bad habits at Christmas continue to have the same bad habits throughout the year. And of course, the credit card companies are eagerly waiting to help. If you get behind on your payments, the card company sends you a nice little reminder, together with advertisements for additional purchases—and sometimes even an offer to increase your credit limit.

If you're like me, each week you get offers from card issuers begging you to sign up for a new card at low introductory rates. All you have to do to activate the card is call an 800 number, speak to a stranger who knows nothing about your financial circumstances, and you're good to go. Another credit card is tempting, but don't do it. For most Americans, credit card purchases have become a sad way of life. Debt has become a resounding curse on sound family financial planning.

GAMBLING WITH CREDIT CARDS

Millions of vacationers travel annually into Las Vegas, Atlantic City, Shreveport, and other gambling locations throughout the country, hoping to hit a big payoff. Some of these travelers openly admit to expecting big winnings to pay off existing credit card debt. To a household with sound financial philosophies, such an expectation may sound crazy, but unfortunately, the hope is a stated fact.

What these vacationers don't realize is that Las Vegas—and every other gambling area—has been built on the principle that *gamblers lose*. Casinos make money because they pay out less than they take in. Does that surprise you? This straightforward strategy generated $32.4 billion in revenues at U.S. commercial casinos in 2006, and $25.5 billion that same year in revenue from gambling enterprises on tribal lands. Casinos are in the business of getting as much of your money as possible while making you feel good about the experience. The next time you visit Las Vegas, observe the gamblers at the tables drinking free alcohol, betting wildly, and trudging back and forth to the cashier's window, using their credit cards to finance more gambling.

Many of us have listened patiently to the exciting stories of the last trip's winnings without asking about the many losing ventures at the same game. Have you noticed that details about prior losses always seem to be rather vague? If gamblers were truly successful at winning, they wouldn't leave the casino. It's sad to watch.

CREDIT CARD COMPANIES: FRIEND OR FOE?

I commented earlier about maxing out your credit cards and not being able to raise your limit whenever you wanted. Well, there's more to the story. When consumers reach their credit card limit, common sense would suggest that the issuer would immediately restrict the use of the card from additional purchases. But that doesn't happen, does it? The reason is that card issuers make more money when you go over your limit by charging you higher interest and fees. Many card issuers have clauses that allow them to hike your interest rate when you go over your limit.

So here you are, already deep in card debt; you've reached your limit, and the card issuer charges you even more interest, plunging you deeper into debt. And here's how the card companies and banks rationalize this practice: because purchases on credit cards are by choice, the card user can stop any time, pay down the balance, and eliminate the higher interest rates or charges on the excess amount. But you know, once the credit card habit is part of your lifestyle, it's hard to kick—even when you reach your card limit. These companies are betting that you won't stop spending once you reach your limit, because higher rates and fees make card issuers a ton of money. Of course, the loser in all this is you. In many cases, you have no idea the bank is charging a higher rate on the increased balance, because the additional amount is buried among all the other charges.

So what is the common sense answer to all this madness? Stay within your limit. Learn to restrain your emotional buying habits. Think before you make that next purchase on your card. Wise families think seriously about making any credit card purchase they can't pay off in one month.

Years ago, I met a fellow in his late forties who told me he was sending his two sons to college on credit cards. He spent several hours each month moving funds from one credit card to another, and since the companies were issuing pre-approved cards by the millions, the process never caught up with him. Following the boys' graduation, he declared bankruptcy and walked away from the debt. A short time later the companies issued him more pre-approved cards.

REMEMBER THE 1980S CREDIT CARD TRAP

The 1980s were an incredible time for credit card companies. Revolving credit and credit card debt skyrocketed from
$55.1 billion in 1980 to $238.6 billion in 1990. This is a 333%
increase in credit card debt in just ten years. Between 1980
and 1990, the number of credit cards more than doubled, and
the average household credit card balance rose from $518 to
nearly $2,700. That was a sizeable increase by any standard,
but more craziness was on the horizon.

Card issuers, observing the country's wild buying habits,
started an aggressive campaign of mailing pre-approved cards
to potential users. Yes, pre-approved cards. The timing couldn't
have been better. Consumers were purchasing goods and services as fast as they could be delivered. At the same time, young
children were watching hours of TV sponsored by companies
advertising new toys and games. Parents, responding to the
children's pleas, bought the new toys on credit as quickly as
they could carry them from the stores. Within weeks, the toys
were broken or thrown in the trash, but the monthly credit
card bills lived on.

Look around you. Aren't many Americans doing the same
thing today?

How long can this go on before credit card problems
destroy a family? For many Americans, the concern is not
just that the family will be financially unstable but the stress
from arguments and self-doubt can damage the family, lead
to bankruptcy, and ultimately bring on divorce. Don't let this
happen to you. It's time to evaluate your financial health and

create a clear family plan to avoid making bad financial decisions in the future.

FAMILY FINANCIAL PLANNING CAN HELP YOU MAKE IT

Family financial planning can be as simple or as complicated as you want to make it. For those of you who prefer the simple approach, here is a plan that won't fail: Pay off all credit card debt as quickly as possible. Attack the ones with the highest interest rate first. For some, due to income levels, this may mean getting a temporary second or third job and dedicating that income to debt reduction. I had three jobs when I first got married, simply to avoid credit card debt. Sit down as a family and discuss the problem, think and pray about it, but get started now—pay off those cards. Pay them off.

THE VALUE OF CASH

A teacher was overheard telling her students, "If you don't learn how to sign your name, you'll have to pay cash for everything."

When I was young, most people carried cash, at least for small everyday purchases. Today, however, we have a different shopping approach. The new process doesn't include cash. We can buy everything from gas to burgers to movie tickets without having folded paper in our pockets.

And that's part of the problem. In this new credit economy, it's difficult to teach our children the value of money, saving, and investing, because money has become an intangible. Money and debt are simply a mystical number on a checking account or credit card billing statement.

Years ago, money was paper bills or coins in our purse or wallet. Now, children rarely see cash, so they don't participate in the family discussions about how much an item costs. With the widespread use of credit cards, children lose the relationship of currency to the real cost of the item. Purchases on credit cards are so easy that many shoppers spend more time on product features than they do on evaluating the price, use, and the real need for the particular item. With a child raised in this family environment, the true value and cost of an item are very difficult to understand.

The Credit Card Review

Try this simple exercise: When your monthly credit card statement arrives, sit down with your children and review each item on the statement. Explain the actual cost of each purchase, why the family needed it, what it's used for, and what, if any, benefit your family receives from the item today. You may be hard-pressed to explain that you are making payments for a broken toy or game or the expensive dinner you ate two weeks ago.

Next, show your children the ongoing interest charges and fees to be paid by your family for those items. And then explain how you're going to pay the bill. Maybe you will do the right thing by paying the entire card balance in one payment.

Maybe you have decided to make monthly payments with interest charges. Or maybe you're forced to make minimum payments. Each monthly statement brings choices. Of course, the strangest conversation would be the one where you are trying to explain why you are using one credit card to pay for another credit card.

If you choose to make monthly payments, show your children the monthly fees on the unpaid balance. Teach them how to allocate the fees to each item and then add these fees onto the original cost. The true cost of each purchase can be downright shocking when the payments are spread over twelve to twenty-four months. A daily latte that cost $3.50 becomes $5.80 with monthly interest and fees. You can make the same drink at home for around twenty cents.

Another approach is to find out how much the item will ultimately cost in added interest and bank charges if you don't pay it off this month. How much next month? And finally, have a discussion about all the items you purchased. Did you truly need them at the time of purchase, or did you simply want them? When you compare wants to needs, the bad habits surface immediately.

SOME OF OUR BAD HABITS

This section about bad buying habits is critical to family financial planning. Those costly habits distract us from making wise decisions. The first thing to recognize is that *needs* are different from *wants*. You need water to live, but you don't need expensive bottled water purchased with a credit card. What are you thinking? Bottled water costs $10 a gallon—more than three times the cost of gasoline. It's interesting to watch people stop for fuel, purchase a plastic bottle of water for $1, and complain about the cost of gasoline as they fill their tank!

Skeptics are calling the bottled-water industry a Great American Hoax, and it's hard not to recognize a kernel of truth in this sentiment. To the shock of many, Earthlings have used spigot water for decades and experienced longevity. Years ago, some members of the bottled water industry financed a study that recommended Americans drink eight glasses of water each day. The recommendation sounded reasonable, even scientific, and the whole country, including the medical community, fell for it. More recent studies tell us the report was flawed.

Read backwards "Evian" spells "naïve."

In reviewing your credit card statements, did you need all the items you purchased this month, or could you have waited until the credit card balance had been paid off? This common sense question brings the element of responsibility into the equation.

A review process is another huge opportunity to sharpen the financial-decision knife. Explain to your children why you didn't use cash. If the answer is that you didn't have the money—the cash—then explain why you decided to make the purchase anyhow. This explanation is going to be tough, but you and your children will learn a great lesson in basic economics that could change your lives forever. Reviewing your credit cards each month with the entire family is an effective tool for teaching your children better money management and the true value of money.

"I have no plan!"

5

Avoid Bad Habits

> People want to be better. Often, they just don't know how.

Bad habits die hard, particularly the habit of buying things we want rather than need. If your habits aren't conducive to making wise decisions, then it's time to reconsider those habits and create new ones. Your life will change for the better. If doing the right thing isn't easy given your current lifestyle, then it's time to change your lifestyle. That's pretty straightforward, isn't it? But the answer really is that simple. Avoiding bad financial decisions can be a lifelong struggle for many Americans. The reason is that good financial decisions and sound retirement planning may require major changes in lifestyle habits, and some of those changes may be hard to make.

Bad Habit #1—Buying Too Much Car

The biggest family budget buster may be sitting in your driveway. In the last ten years, as the price of new vehicles rose substantially, salaries remained flat. Isn't food on the table more important that driving a flashy car?

The next time you take a leisure drive, cruise by your local car dealer. You'll notice there are more car buying options than ever before. Size, shape, color, horsepower, and a wide range of new features such as keyless entry, rear-seat DVD players, window tint, additional power outlets for laptops and electric devices. . . . The list goes on and on.

What began as a necessity, transporting us around town or across the country, has changed into a status symbol and, at the same time, a very expensive adult toy. The American car has an almost storybook past. In October 1908, Henry Ford produced the first Model T and sold it for $950. Perhaps Ford's greatest contribution was the moving assembly line. First introduced at the Highland Park, Michigan, plant in 1913, the assembly line allowed autoworkers to stay in one place as the cars, in various manufacturing stages, passed by.

In 1929, Paul Galvin, head of Galvin Manufacturing Corporation, invented the first car radio. In 1940, Packard offered the first car with an air-conditioning system. In 1948, we got electric windows. Then in the 1950s, with GM in the lead, cars got bigger and more powerful, and at the same time easier to drive. The American car of the '50s was considered the best in the world for the money. And of course the '50s were a time when speed, horsepower, and comfort were synonymous with youth.

When I was nineteen, I bought a new '57 Chevy. Several of my friends helped me modify the engine to add more power, loud mufflers, and chrome exhaust pipes. It had a red and black interior with a customized chrome dash. Everyone in the neighborhood wanted to ride in it, just to listen to the mufflers roar. I gave all comers a ride, secretly hoping that after I wooed them with the power and the noise they wouldn't complain about the muffler sound when I came home at night. My new car was a very expensive toy, and I loved it dearly. Coming from a low-income neighborhood, it made me feel like a cool guy.

In the 1950s and 1960s, cars were selling as fast as they rolled off the assembly line. But then something happened. The increase in car prices began to outpace family incomes. In the 1970s, the average price of a car was $17,200. In the 1980s, it jumped to $21,200. And in the 1990s, the average car price rose to $23,300. Today, the average price is $28,400. A new car is second only to a home as the most expensive purchase for most consumers.

Studies tell us that auto buyers in Dallas and Houston, where the big SUV reigns supreme, have the highest average vehicle payments in the country: we're talking $500 or more each month. In my opinion, payments that high should be reserved for a mortgage. These enormous auto payments can result in family conflicts over money and may eventually lead to bankruptcies.

All this struggle and effort over a wasting asset! The very day you drive your new car or truck home, it depreciates 20% to 40%, depending on the make and model. Imagine how upset you would be if your 401(k) lost 20 to 40% in one day. On a $30,000 vehicle, you've lost $6,000 to $12,000 on the drive from the dealership to your driveway. Wow! Do you make that much money that you can afford to absorb such a loss? Second-year depreciation typically runs 10% to 15%. The third year, it's another 10% to 15%.

When a vehicle gets to be two or three years old, many owners want to trade up for something new. To motivate trade-ins, dealers offer "special financing" to get us into a new car. But guess what? This new financing typically increases the payment for the next three to five years. At some point, the upward spiral of higher payments leads to a financial collapse, because salaries don't increase at the same rate.

Even before trading up to a new car, many car owners are already "upside down" with the equity in the car. Being "upside down" means that you owe more money than the car is worth. This is another recipe for disaster. Making large monthly payments on a depreciating asset puts a strain on the monthly budget and can be emotionally draining as long as you own or lease the vehicle. The question before you is which is more important, your family or your truck? If you even have to think about it, this is a good time to look at your priorities.

Automakers are in the business of selling cars and trucks. To be successful, they've come up with some imaginative selling tactics. Financing options include zero-down loans, zero-percent interest, preapproved loans, and cash incentives. Some new car sales promotions send you out the door with a new vehicle and cash in your hand. The new found cash can be used for upgrades on your new car, a shopping spree, or paying off outstanding credit card debt. Many buyers are so excited at the thought of getting a new car and walking away with cash that they completely forget the higher monthly payments, sometimes increasing by as much as $500 per month, for the length of the loan. Whatever happened to my friend "Common Sense" and 1 + 1 = 2?

When new car financing specials don't sell enough cars, the automakers use another effective advertising strategy—they get you hooked on horsepower. How does that work? They encourage you to take it for a drive. Take it home if you like and really get a feel for all that power. What a rush it brings as you drive through the neighborhood, hoping to impress people you don't even know. Current television advertising shows cars and trucks racing down the highway with huge engines.

Today, most auto manufacturers have mammoth engine designs on their drawing boards for the American market, while the same car designers have smaller, fuel-efficient engines for the rest of the world. These enormous engines consume huge amounts of expensive premium gasoline while most drivers complain openly about the price of fuel. For most of us, buying a car for the added horsepower doesn't make any sense. Many of these super-powered cars spend much of their time driving ten miles per hour in rush-hour traffic.

Everyone wants to feel important, and maybe a shiny new car is their fifteen minutes of fame. Instead of those fleeting moments, how about foregoing the new car and experiencing a lifetime of wise decisions resulting in financial security and family wealth?

Here's a neat idea for saving money and getting the car or truck you need—the next time you're looking for a new car or truck, consider buying a used one. Purchase it from a reputable dealer, preferably the dealer who sold it originally. The manager of the used car section can provide that information to you. Before you buy anything, contact the Better Business Bureau and ask about consumer complaints at that dealership. This information is another check to help you make an informed decision.

Once you've decided on the age, make, and model, familiarize yourself with your state's anti-lemon laws. Ask if the vehicle has ever been in an accident, get the answer in writing, and request that the original warranty remain in place. Some additional research might include reading about the car in *Consumer Reports*. Look at old issues to see what consumers thought of the car when it was new, and then look up the latest issue to see what they think of it today.

After the purchase, keep the car for four to five years and repeat the procedure. Many buyers follow this approach and swear by the long-term results both for owning a high quality car and for making the most of their working assets. In fact, many employees of car dealers particularly mechanics are constantly on the lookout for these types of cars that come into the lot as trade-ins. They understand the real value of the vehicle and the right price to be paid for it.

Bad Habit #2 — Auto Leasing

When the debate about buying versus leasing is put on the table, jugular veins immediately swell. Everyone has an opinion, so let's take a close look at what really happens. What's the biggest vehicle expense in the first three years of ownership (which coincidentally is the most common time frame for auto leasing)? Is it gasoline, oil, maintenance, tires, washing, or insurance? Wrong. As discussed above, the biggest expense is depreciation.

Yep, you heard it right. Depreciation measures the car's

loss in value from the moment you drive it off the showroom floor. Depreciation means your car or truck is worth less today than it was yesterday, last month, or last year. Automobiles are a wasting asset. Period! And while that is basic information, most auto owners don't think about it, won't accept it, and refuse to consider depreciation as a factor in the car-buying decision.

Leasing companies will tell you that you only pay for what you use and that you'll always have a new vehicle to impress your co-workers and neighbors. Further, your monthly payments are smaller with a lease. But when you apply the same question to owning or renting a home, a different answer surfaces.

Wealth builders know that the path to success is through ownership of assets. If you lease cars and rent homes all your life, where is your wealth? At the end of your journey, you have nothing except cancelled checks. You don't even own a garage, let alone anything to put in it.

Whether you lease or buy, it's important to treat all your assets with a high level of importance. If someone told you to leave your $25,000 fur coat outside on the driveway each night, you wouldn't consider it. A fur coat is too valuable to treat it that way. So why do you pay $25,000 or more for a car and park it outside in the driveway, fading the paint, drying out the rubber parts, and destroying the upholstery?

What's the difference between your fur coat and your auto? None at all. Both are valuable, both can be damaged by the elements, and both require reasonable care. We leave our cars parked in the drive or on the street out of laziness, convenience, or both. Owners who take this approach accelerate the loss in value by not taking care of their cars. It's not long before the car no longer looks good, which motivates them to buy vehicles more frequently, creating higher ongoing car debt. Get the picture?

Bad Habit #3—The Wrong Investments

We know how the media likes to poke fun at politicians and celebrities for their foolish antics. They love to report stories about the toys these celebs buy and never use—items like unoccupied mansions, vineyards, dozen of cars, and herds of cattle or bison that wander aimlessly on large tracts of land. They buy Arabian show horses that have never known a saddle. They acquire deserted land in the middle of nowhere. The list goes on. Most who have heard these bizarre stories wonder how many ways that wealth could have been put to a better use.

I mention these celebrity events as one example of emotional craziness and bad financial habits that should be avoided. But celebrities aren't the only ones who make bad decisions. In Texas, where I live, for years there were television advertisements about a get-rich-quick scheme involving the breeding of emus. An emu, for those who don't know, is the second-largest bird in the world by height, after its relative, the ostrich. The ads told us that if we moved quickly, we could "get in on the ground level" of an "emerging industry." The exploding demand for emu products such as leather, oil, and low-fat, low-cholesterol meat would be out of sight. Only it didn't happen, and the Texas emu industry has all but dried up.

Emu growers, frustrated by their losing ventures, turned their birds loose in the middle of the night to wander the countryside. In some cases, breeders slaughtered entire flocks. Most emu speculators went broke feeding another failed fad. You may be surprised to learn that many of them had paid—hold on to your hat—$20,000 for eggs with something unknown inside a shell! Now that's flat-out crazy, no matter how much money you have. Many wealthy Texans were duped by this whacky scheme.

Do you remember the strange appeal of Cabbage Patch dolls in the early 1980s and Beanie Babies in the mid 1990s? Now that really was speculative nonsense. People bought the dolls because they expected to make a killing within a short period of time. Even today, many of these folks have attics, garages, and basements full of these dolls, hoping someday they will be worth more than what they paid for them. That money could have been used in so many better investments. What were they thinking?

Now, if that's not bad enough, during that wild period when the dolls were being placed on the store shelves, there were ugly TV stories showing women having fistfights over which one was going to buy the doll. They were going berserk over a *doll*! You wouldn't believe it unless you actually saw it. Absolutely crazy! And why did they do it? Because of a false promise that the dolls were going to be worth a lot of money some day.

Another ongoing speculative venture is the purchase of limited-edition coins. Here are the questions: who is buying these coins, and what are they going to do with them? Apparently many misguided souls are buying this stuff, because each Sunday our local newspaper prints an expensive, full-page ad for the latest weekly offer of a "special, limited-edition" coin that has no value other than its small metal content. But readers evidently buy them to be stored in a safety-deposit box in the bank, creating yet another unnecessary cost to the family. As they purchase more and more of the coins—yes, you guessed it—they rent a bigger, more costly box at the bank.

Folks, this is not sound financial planning by any measure. In fact, this is not financial planning at all. How much monthly income will the coins produce in retirement? How will you use them to achieve your financial goals? Just another broken fad. Starting to get the picture? It's not a pretty one. No one else will buy the coins from you at any price. If anyone can buy the same fad items at the "low" advertised price, who would have a good reason to buy yours at a higher price? Some people just never get it.

Wise investors diligently avoid bad investments

Bad Habit #4—Watching Too Much Financial Television

While many retirees keep themselves very busy, some men spend much of their day in front of the TV watching the financial news. This phenomenon is what I call the "green arrow, red arrow" syndrome. When the financial markets move up, the ticker shows a little green arrow; down, a little red arrow. Unfortunately for some, the color of the arrow reflects more than the current direction of the markets. A red arrow means bad news, and repeated bad news can lead to depression, anxiety, and even poor health. The effect of too much financial news and inactivity could result in stress, resulting in medical problems more serious than a fluctuating stock market.

Let me take a moment to address the wives of men who suffer this syndrome. Ladies, please realize that when your husband can't pull himself away from the TV, it means he is worried and insecure about the markets. And worse, he doesn't trust anyone but himself to look after these important matters. In many instances, he doesn't even trust you. Nowadays, of course, we know better—my own daughters are proof—but many older men were taught that they, and they alone, make the decisions about money, even though many secretly admit they don't understand the financial markets.

So how do you address this daily ordeal? My suggestion, and I say this only half-jokingly, is to go out. Leave the house and take the remote control with you. When you return home, you might be surprised to find a husband who is strangely calm and conversant. Another approach is to replace the batteries in the remote control with dead ones. This will temporarily cure the problem. Your job then is to quickly reintroduce yourself to your husband and try to bring sanity back to his life. Tell him you miss him and want to spend more time with him. Whatever method you choose, be sure to wean him slowly.

"Our plan is working!"

6

How to Plan for Your Retirement

If you planned for only twenty-five years of retirement, what happens if you live for thirty?

In 1994, Barbara, an energetic woman in her early forties came to my office to start an investment program for retirement. She began the discussion by telling me her uncle warned her not to invest in the stock market because he lost all his money in the crash of 1929. He recommended that she put all of her money in CDs. I asked how old her uncle was and she said he was 74. I asked if she was sure of his age and she talked about celebrating his birthday two weeks ago. I rose from my chair to put some numbers on the office blackboard.

I said if he is now 74, he was born in 1920 and was only nine years old during the stock market meltdown of 1929. Obviously, he had no money to invest and was too young to be a legal investor. She looked at me and said, "Why would he make up such a story?"

I told her that her uncle was probably well-intentioned, but to many older folks who consider themselves survivors of the Great Depression, the stock market represents nothing more than Wall Street's version of Las Vegas. They experience the fear of the unknown. Today's investment environment is something they don't understand, and they caution others to take a skeptical view. I explained that Wall Street is one of the most regulated investing environments in the world, and I took the time to discuss current risk/reward models and how they could help Barbara make wise investment decisions that fit her risk tolerance. Barbara decided to take the risk and invest in a growth mutual fund for the potential to invest in the great companies in America that would reward her at a higher level than the small amount she could make in bank CDs.

LIFE CYCLES BRING CHANGES

If you are in your twenties, when the subject of retirement comes up, you probably roll your eyes and find the discussion either humorous or boring. In your thirties, the word retirement raises minimal interest. In your forties, however, retirement starts to become a major source of concern, and if you haven't started an investment plan by your fifties, the mention of retirement gives you a stomachache. You start to worry if you'll be part of that small group of Americans that will enjoy a comfortable retirement. In your sixties, the anxiety over retirement planning can be overwhelming, resulting in high blood pressure and serious health problems.

If this sounds exaggerated, I can assure you I know this sequence to be accurate from the many conversations with my clients. Retirement and financial security can be a wonderful experience for all who take advantage of the ways to plan and invest. Financial security in retirement means being able to maintain the same lifestyle after you quit working. In a country like America, filled with so many incredible opportunities, why would anyone work forty to fifty years and not commit to monthly investing for a comfortable retirement? Perhaps, as an alternative, they are planning on a short life?

Get the Family Involved

In most older families, only one spouse assumes responsibility for selecting and monitoring savings or investment statements. The other spouse assumes no responsibility, but usually has plenty of comments on the subject. I jokingly tell my clients that there are two kinds of people who complain about money—men and women. When was the last time you openly said you have enough in your investments?

I strongly recommend a simple exercise to see if both husband and wife are on the same page with respect to financial planning. I suggest that each spouse go into a separate room and take a notepad with them. Each should list the top five financial challenges that need to be addressed in the near future. They exchange lists and look at the common items and those that differ. You may be surprised by the goals of your spouse, and you may also learn more about what they really want out of life. This exercise can be helpful in aligning your financial goals and helping create or reinforce the family financial plan.

Retirement Planning For Living Longer

Most of us want a long life. In 1900, the life expectancy in America was 45 to 47 years old. In 2000, the life expectancy was 75 to 80. Modern medical techniques, drugs, therapy, and surgery have changed the way we think about aging. As we consider our prospective futures, the question is how to estimate realistic life spans so that our investments match or survive them and that is not an easy task.

Obviously you want to be sure your retirement income generators, (also known as investments) have a life span as long as you do. Of course, family lineage plays a big part in the equation. In fact, many researchers think we can use our grandparents' and parents' ages to develop a reasonable assumption for our life expectancy.

As a good source, we look to the life insurance companies and their actuary tables to assist us in a basic approach for calculating meaningful life expectancies. Excluding accidental death, we can average the ages of our parents at the time of their deaths, and if we didn't smoke, use a lot of alcohol or drugs, or struggle with weight issues or diabetes, we can add five to ten years to the numbers.

If our parents died at 66 and 96, the average age at death is 81 (66 + 96 divided by 2). We then add five to ten years and have a potential life expectancy of 86 to 91. Is it absolute? Of course not. As in all life-expectancy tables, it's an estimate, but that number can be very useful in the approach to investment strategies designed to sustain a certain lifestyle. We don't want to be long on life and short on money at age 60, 70, or 80.

Retirement Planning Dos And Don'ts

Many worthless seminars and books suggest that if you work just a few hours each week in your home, you will become rich. Unless you have the magic formula to eliminate male baldness, a few hours of work won't make you financially secure. It's not going to happen. Only those speakers and authors who travel the country presenting these outlandish schemes or writing books for a huge fee will cash in. Family retirement planning and wealth building take more than a few hours, but it's not impossible. I've created a list of Dos and Don'ts, which I hope you find helpful in your planning process.

Planning Dos

1. **Learn the fundamental difference between savings and investments.** Having that important information will help you place your money in the appropriate financial programs. Understand how long-term rates of return for savings and investing can differ significantly and could affect your ability to retire and stay retired at a predetermined age.

2. **Start a monthly investment plan in a properly diversified growth and income program.** One good approach is known as dollar-cost-averaging, investing a level amount each month through payroll deductions in an employer-sponsored retirement plan. You can also invest on your own, using the same strategy, through monthly investing into many different types of programs that match your risk/reward goals.

3. **Develop long-term financial strategies for retiring.** You can think short-term when you put your money in CDs, money markets, and credit unions, but think long-term (five years or more) about investment performance, because market fluctuations can influence your potential rate of return and monthly income in retirement. Consider new, guaranteed-income programs, known as living benefits, offered through annuities. Many offerings of these programs with various benefits and features are available. If you consider them, be sure to read the prospectus that explains how the program is structured.

4. **Always invest in programs that can produce monthly income to support your lifestyle in retirement.** Become familiar with the various programs that offer systematic monthly withdrawals and how they can best fit your circumstances. Individual stocks that provide 1.5% dividend per year are not meaningful to a retiree who wants to withdraw 5% each year. The extra amount of income required to maintain a lifestyle could only be achieved through the constant sale of stocks and resulting high commissions, which will quickly erode the effectiveness of the portfolio.

5. **Have realistic expectations about the future performance of your investments.** Many investors anticipate such lofty performance levels that the family financial plan becomes ineffective due to under investing.

6. **Avoid anything, including rental homes, that you have to feed on a regular basis.** That includes livestock and other animals unless, of course, you just want to be a rancher. These types of investments may require enormous amounts of ongoing capital to support their potential for future income. Talk to the many frustrated investors in Texas who have set their money-losing emus loose throughout the state!

7. **Things that glitter are not investments.** Jewelry does not produce monthly retirement income. I have met many who are adamant about buying jewelry. Before you argue the point, how much monthly income can you get from a $25,000 watch? A life of accumulating such items without directing your money into income-generating working assets can spell disaster in retirement.

8. **Review your savings and investment account balances monthly to measure your asset growth progress.** Your constant awareness brings a keen eye to what's working. But be patient with your research. When you have more than one investment, they will perform at different levels. If you have ten different programs, one will be the best, one will be the worst, and the rest will be somewhere in between. Patient observation might show that the top one may fall into the middle of the performance range next year and the lowest has moved up in the order. Experienced investors learn to understand how investments can fluctuate yearly to establish an overall, long-term, acceptable performance goal.

9. **Enjoy your family wealth.** There is nothing morally wrong with having lots of money if you earned it legally. Most people work for years to accumulate wealth and cherish the confidence it brings in their lives. Their satisfaction is not the same feeling as that realized by inherited wealth, which requires only that you show up.

10. **Pay off credit card debt each month and live beneath your means.** This is a simple equation; credit card debt equals living beyond your income. Many Americans do not know how to spend less than they earn, but this approach can directly affect how quickly you build your retirement accounts and achieve financial security.

11. **If you don't have the experience, time, or commitment to research the financial markets for investment information, develop a long-term relationship with a trusted financial advisor.** It's common knowledge that those with substantial wealth employ one or more advisors to help manage their family investments, taxes, and estate planning. If you don't have the expertise, call in the experts.

12. **Become familiar with your employer retirement plan.** The lack of participation by employees in 401(k), 403(b), and 457 plans is a bad habit for most families. But it's never too late to contact the proper department to start your program. Complete the forms as soon as possible, and commit to understanding the plan, the special tax benefits, and how much you can contribute each pay period. Planning is that simple, but procrastination kills success.

Planning Don'ts

1. **Don't forget to diversify.** Placing all your money in the same kind of account, such as CDs, but at different banks, is not diversification. It's just extra work.

2. **Don't over-diversify. Thirty or more mutual funds are not a form of diversification.** It's a paperwork nightmare befitting those who have too much time on their hands. Most folks want their lives simplified. Proper diversification is a time-tested method for a family plan.

3. **Don't use savings accounts as your only wealth-building option.** Limiting your goals to low monthly income from CDs, money market funds, and credit unions without consideration for total return is a bad habit. The goal for a successful investment program is long-term growth and income.

4. **Don't speculate. Invest.** There's a big difference. Speculating in high-risk current fads (Beanie Babies, Cabbage Patch dolls, heavily promoted coins, emus, baseball cards, old cars, art collections, and gun collections) can be a recipe for failure. These are not income generators, these are hobbies.

5. **Don't slip into "paralysis from analysis" that is the result of spending too much time on unnecessary research and using that wasted time as an excuse for not investing.** A frequent question is "When should I invest?" The answer is "When you have money," because there isn't a bad time to make a good investment.

6. **Don't panic when the media makes big stories over nothing.** Panicking when your portfolio temporarily goes down is emotionally harmful to the entire family. Most investments, especially stocks, experience daily price fluctuations. Those movements, when properly managed, can be an opportunity for significant performance in the long-term growth and income of your account.

7. **Don't overreact to taxes.** Too much concern about capital gains tax can keep you from making good financial decisions. Avoiding capital gains is one of the most common reasons offered by uninformed investors for not selling individual stocks when they should be repositioned to establish a properly diversified investment strategy that can generate dependable monthly income.

8. **Don't pay taxes until they are due.** If you have to pay tax on your capital gain, then you made a profit. Isn't that the specific reason for investing? But paying ordinary income taxes on money you are not using, such as the interest earned on CDs, money markets, and credit unions, is a bad habit. Say this several times, and it will become part of your financial planning: "Don't pay income taxes each year on money you are not using." Talk to your advisor about the benefits of tax-free and tax-deferred programs to discover the tax advantages that you may be missing.

9. **Don't be too cautious.** Thinking primarily of safety rather than long-term growth and income can dramatically

reduce your overall portfolio performance and future monthly retirement income.

10. **Don't believe the braggarts.** Successful investors usually are quiet about their money. Avoid investments discussed at cocktail parties that supposedly provide extraordinary, tax-free returns that are 100% liquid and without risk. These investments don't exist.

11. **Don't hesitate to make prudent decisions.** Unload your bad investments now.

And Here Is a Repeat:
Three Necessary Steps to Financial Security

1. Get out of credit card and auto debt and start a monthly investment program.

2. Get out of credit card and auto debt and start a monthly investment program.

3. Get out of credit card and auto debt and start a monthly investment program.

"My good advice is working for you."

7

Wealthy Investors Have Advisors

We all live under the same sky, but we don't have the same horizons.

Several years ago, Betty, an elderly client, called my office to bring something important to my attention. She had just received an account statement and noticed someone had withdrawn money from a tax-free mutual fund she jointly owned with her husband through my firm. She wanted me to find out what happened. Betty said she didn't request or receive a check, and she went as far as suggesting that maybe someone in my office had taken money from her account. Frankly, I was stunned by the accusation.

I immediately called the mutual fund company to determine if a withdrawal had been made, how much, when, and who requested the withdrawal. I was advised that her husband had recently withdrawn $5,000 from their joint mutual fund. I called Betty and told her so. Thinking the worst, she went ballistic. While I was listening on the phone, she asked her husband if he had made a withdrawal, and he acknowledged he had.

The rest of the conversation turned ugly. Betty's husband wanted to know who she was talking to, and when he realized it was me, he took the phone and apologized to me for his wife's rude behavior. He explained to both of us that he had withdrawn the funds to pay for a surprise anniversary trip. They were leaving later that week for a ten-day cruise. Betty started crying, then got on the phone and told me she knew all along that we would never take any of her money.

Without an advisor, Betty would probably have come unraveled trying to find out who took money from their account.

As a young man, I enjoyed reading financial magazines and listening to stories of those who had accumulated or managed great wealth. These were giants of industry, investment gurus, single-minded visionaries, and Wall Street winners. They sounded to me very much like financial heroes. It wasn't long before I noticed a pattern—people who generated substantial wealth had financial advisors. As I followed the stories, I became aware of the advisor's role, which was to offer professional advice on subjects the moguls knew little about. The discovery that these wealthy giants of industry depended on professionals to help them make wise financial decisions was a big surprise.

Selecting a financial advisor is easier than you think. When you are looking for a doctor, dentist, attorney, or accountant, how do you do it? Most of us typically ask our friends and neighbors for suggestions. We want to know who they use and whether they're satisfied with the service and the related fees. The same approach works well for financial advisors. Ask your close friends who their financial advisor is, what investments they are in, the performance of their accounts, how they pay for the service, and whether the advisor is informative during the annual office visits.

When you have selected an advisor, use focused questions to decide on a specific investment program. You should always understand the benefits of each recommendation to determine whether it matches your risk/reward goals. Have a note pad to write down all the important information. Discuss your long-term goals. Be sure to express your concern for growth, growth and income, and the safety of your invested principal.

Ask who will review your investments each year and who makes the specific recommendations for your portfolio. Get to know that person on the first visit. Smart investors always monitor the success of their investment program with their advisor at least once a year. This can be achieved through an office visit, email, or phone calls, but an annual financial checkup is as important as an annual medical checkup. The review indicates a level of interest that is important to both the client and the advisor. The visits should also be enjoyable as you learn from each conversation why you are invested in a particular program. If you have investments with a bank or a mutual fund, ask how frequently the personnel will contact you for an investment review. Most banks I am familiar with don't talk to investors again following the transaction. Mutual funds operate the same way. But your money, just like your health, deserves ongoing attention.

What Is Your Source for Financial Advice?

Financial magazines, newspapers, and subscription periodicals are in business to sell copy. Higher sales mean higher profits. As an investor, if you make or lose money due to information found in these sources, it's purely coincidental. For years, financial magazines have presented the "Top 20 Mutual Funds" or the "50 Best Stocks" or the "Global 100" as a teaser on the cover. If these are the best stocks or funds, why does the list change every year? The answer is that change attracts readers. If the journalists knew these were going to be high-performing accounts, don't you think they would have invested all their money in them? Don't you think they'd be sitting on the back porch right now, counting their earnings? What you are getting in the magazine is prior performance numbers. Anyone can get that information because it is history. Smart investors must properly allocate their accounts for future performance.

My concern with these news sources is that they encourage investors to disregard proper asset allocation. It's tempting to read about the "Best Stocks or Mutual Funds of 2007" and, on impulse, add several of these top picks to your portfolio. The problem is that if you follow this poor advice for several years, you will end up owning 200 to 300 different stocks and mutual funds, which becomes a recipe for disaster. It's confusing, it's a tax nightmare, and it's unnecessary.

Bad Sources for Advice

Consider when questionable claims turn into outlandish promises. At a cocktail party you hear about a new investment that includes a hedge fund, futures, split shares, options, or maybe a wild offshore investment earning 20% per year, tax free, 100% liquid, with no risk. Friends at the party are a little hazy on the details, but tell you they all made a killing in only six months. As you drive home . . . you wonder about everyone else making easy money and why you aren't. First thing in the morning, you place a phone call to your long-time advisor and tell him you've found a magic way to make unbelievable profits. The response is complete silence, and in those brief moments, you listen to yourself and realize how foolish it sounds. My advice here is not to allow tall tales at the water cooler or a cocktail party stand in the way of your family financial plan. Do it the right way.

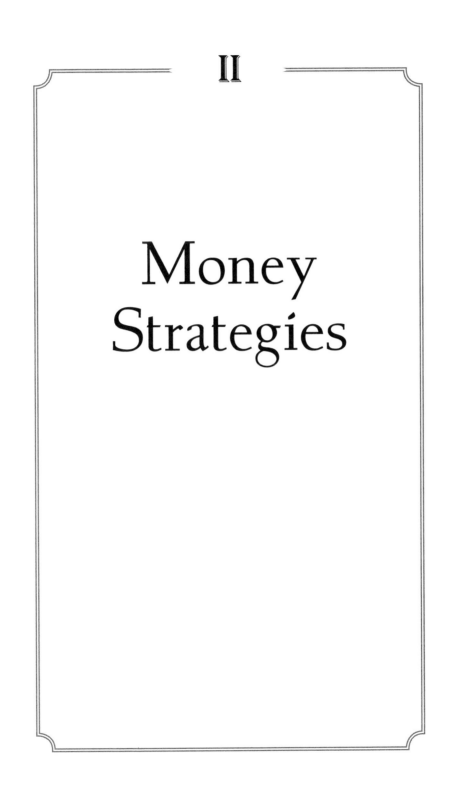

II

Money
Strategies

"There really is a difference."

8

Saving Versus Investing

Some claim it's too expensive to save for retirement.
What exactly does that mean?

In 1990, Margaret, a woman I didn't know, called my office with a request that we meet that day. She wanted to invest in an annuity right away and needed some advice. She had listened to my radio program for several months, liked what I was saying, and thought an annuity would be right for her. I advised her that I was booked most of the day, but she insisted on meeting me as soon as possible, so I made the appointment.

At noon, she arrived carrying a large brown bag, which she held tightly to her chest. At first, I thought it was her lunch. During our short meeting, she told me that she had been married for over twenty years, and, sadly, within the last ten years her husband had started drinking heavily and abusing her.

To earn money, Margaret installed a kiln in her basement where she made ceramic dolls to be sold at outdoor markets. It took a while, but Margaret had accumulated more than $10,000. In her purse she had a one-way ticket to California, where she planned to live with her sister and start a new life.

Then she reached into the big brown paper bag and removed what looked like a large brick wrapped in aluminum foil. She placed the aluminum block on the glass top table in my office. A strange white substance started to appear on the glass surrounding the large pile. I looked at her, trying to figure out what was happening.

She explained that she hid the money from her husband by wrapping it in aluminum foil and burying it in a pile deep within her freezer. The aluminum block was literally "cold cash." She peeled back the aluminum and started spreading the packets of frozen bills across the table. The white covering immediately expanded across the table. The money was wrapped with rubber bands in bundles containing various denominations—$10, $20, $50, and $100.

Margaret was determined to make a better life for herself, and over the years she had created her own personal financial plan. An important part of that new life required saving and investing in order to change her future. Saving money can be difficult, but if a person like Margaret can do it, you can too.

Did You Have the Sacred Envelopes?

Those born in the 1940s and earlier might remember how families got along before credit cards. Remember how families used to save money for special occasions? Every week, moms and dads filled specially marked envelopes with cash. Each envelope was labeled for a particular event throughout the year. The envelopes were sacred and placed in a designated drawer. When I was growing up, according to my parents, most of our neighbors had these envelopes in the house. Each family had an envelope for Christmas, Easter, birthday, vacations, back to school, and other major celebrations.

The idea grew out of the Christmas and vacation clubs that banks offered at the time. The plan was to save a little cash each payday and put it in a special account at your local bank. I remember going to the bank each week to make our deposits. Then my mother got the idea she could do it on her own and save herself a bus trip to the bank.

Money was scarce in our home. Each Friday evening when Dad was paid, she placed a few dollars in each envelope. She let us know about the deposit and the current balance as we sat around the dinner table in the kitchen. There were no surprises, and the family budget was firm. You knew how much was put away and what the money would be used for. This was a simple and successful process. No one in the family ever considered borrowing from the funds. It was such a simple plan for financial security.

Surprisingly, in the 1940s and 1950s, most of the country used the same system, and it all worked rather well. The tradition was handed down from one generation to the next. Then the Baby Boomers arrived, and due to the size of the Boomer population—those born between 1946 and 1964—the financial services industry saw an opportunity to offer credit to millions of willing consumers.

As Boomers entered the job market, their financial world changed dramatically. They exceeded the achievements of previous generations, earning more, saving and investing more, and realizing greater family wealth than prior generations. Boomers spent more than any other generation in history, had more credit card debt, and filed more bankruptcies than past generations. And that trend continues today. The Boomer generation disposed of those old-fashioned savings envelopes and replaced them with credit cards. And there goes the simple plan for financial security.

Smart investors recognize that achieving financial security requires a plan that includes saving, investing, and wise money-management techniques. Regardless of how you approach your family financial plan, don't underestimate the wealth-building power of a savings plan.

1. Start by knowing what you want to do with your money, and establish achievable goals and objectives.

2. Save a certain amount each week or month, depending on how frequently you are paid.

3. Review your savings and investment accounts monthly.

4. Know how much you've put in them so you can get a sense of how much your accounts have grown.

5. Get excited about your accounts because you're doing the right thing for your family.

Understand Your Risk/Reward Profile

Investments perform differently from savings because investments are managed without guaranteeing the principal. In an investment, the principal (the original amount you invested) can fluctuate up or down. If the investment is flawed by poor management, you could lose all your money. Through-out the 1990s, investors expected unreasonable returns from their stock investments: up to 20% annually. One reason is that friends and family routinely boasted of unreasonable returns. A balanced portfolio of stocks, bonds, and cash went out of style and was replaced almost exclusively with high-risk/reward fad investments, including the dotcom companies that were overbought through day trading.

For several years during the late 1990s, day trading worked only because the stock markets were rapidly moving upward. In March 2000, the NASDAQ reached an all-time high of 5,132. However, due to a recession in 2000, the washout of technology and dotcom companies, and the terrorist attacks on September 11, 2001, the stock market downturn bot-tomed out in October 2002. The NASDAQ dropped to 1,108, causing investors to lose from their all-time high an average 78% of the value of their stock-related investments. "Dotcom had become "dotbomb." As a result, day traders experienced enormous losses and quit the markets, many suffering severe emotional stress and poor health. For some, the combination was lethal.

Since October 2002, the stock markets have once again created substantial gains for long-term investors. And yes, the conservative, balanced accounts are back in vogue. In hindsight, we look at April 2000 to October 2002 as a bear market—meaning stock values were down 10% or more.

Yield vs. Total Return: Know the Difference

Yield and total return are not the same. *Yield* is the interest paid on bonds, CDs, money markets, passbook savings, and credit union accounts. Yield generally refers to the anticipation of a quoted percentage, such as 3% yield per year. A $100,000 CD with a 3% yield will pay $3,000 of interest per year. *Total return* is the yield plus the fluctuation in the value of the principal due to market conditions. Many brokered CDs have experienced negative total return because the underlying CD lost principal value although it had a stated yield. The yield payment can be dispersed monthly, quarterly, semiannually, or annually, depending on how the program is designed. The investor chooses the payout frequency.

Conservative Expectations

Moderate Expectations

Aggressive Expectations

9

Invest the Way
You Drive

The problem with opportunity is that
it comes disguised as hard work.

In the late 1980s, James and his wife Linda, both aged 65, came to me with an interesting planning challenge. Several years earlier, James and a group of professional friends had started a company to develop a new software product for mass production. James's position was manager of distribution, a title he thought humorous because he was, in fact, the supervisor of the small mailroom. His compensation was $60,000 a year plus a modest health-insurance plan.

The company had no pension plan because it didn't have the capital to fund it. All the employees worked there with the single goal of developing a unique, proprietary product that would dramatically enhance computer memory and speed. The employees hoped that the product would be so effective it would attract a sale of their company to a much larger corporation. Just as planned, a large computer company approached them with an offer, and James's after-tax share of the company was $1.4 million.

He had two questions for me. If he invested the money, how much income could he receive each month? And, of course, how long would it last? I talked to him about the way he drove and how that could be related to a risk/reward investment strategy. He explained that due to poor vision, he usually drove slower than the others did. That told me that conservative programs were more likely to appeal to James. I know it's a different approach, but it is quite effective in determining the level of risk that an investor can handle.

I provided James and Linda with a detailed plan for investing the funds. The plan included a list of investments, expected monthly income, assumed inflation rate, and a schedule detailing how long the principal would last. When we put the numbers together with his Social Security benefits, it was clear James and Linda would receive more monthly income than they currently received in salary. James looked at his wife and asked if he could use my phone. He got up from our meeting, called his office, and told them he was retiring in two weeks.

James and Linda took a big risk investing in a startup company, and it paid off. It's a success story with a happy ending. I believe we can have a happy ending, even if most of us will not have an opportunity to participate in a startup company.

Invest the Way You Drive

Wise investors expect to earn the highest rate of return, within the shortest period of time, with the highest level of safety. This means evaluating the risks and rewards of each investment, and if the anticipated benefits make sense, committing to the selection—that is, you move forward with the investment. There's no question that investing can be risky. As we consider other risks in life, it's a wonder we ever leave our homes. Nearly 50,000 motorists die each year on our highways and close to a million are seriously injured, yet we get behind the wheel anyway. We do it because we know intuitively that if we drive safely on roads in reasonable weather, and without the influence of drugs or alcohol, we can expect to arrive safely.

One of the things I've learned in life is that the aging process negatively affects our ability to handle stress. During the bear markets of 2001 and 2002, I noticed that some investors became emotional about the downward trending stock markets even though they never made withdrawals or planned to make withdrawals in the near future. They just couldn't accept that markets had retreated and they were affected so negatively, if only on paper.

When talking about any type of risk, one of the examples I use with clients is to compare their current approaches to life to the way they acted when they were young. Consider, for example, going on a Jeep ride. When they were young, they wanted the top down, the air blowing in their face, and the radio blaring. They drove down the highway at high speeds, hoping for the thrill of hitting a bump and sailing through the air. But as they got older, their desires for that same Jeep ride became a lot different. Now they want the top secured tightly around them to keep out the sun, road noise, and wind. They want the radio volume much lower, and they have no desire to hit bumps of any size. None! As we grow older, we don't handle life's bumps as well as we used to, and that applies to our investment pursuits.

Here is a highly effective way to consider how to invest your money—invest the way you drive. If you drive slowly, consider offerings that focus on safety rather than growth. If you drive the speed limit, you might consider 60% equities with the remaining 40% income-oriented to bonds. This portfolio could work if you can tolerate some volatility as a trade-off for greater long-term gains that are designed to outpace inflation. Discuss your risk/reward goals with your advisor.

If you drive aggressively, you might consider putting all your money in equities or similar higher risk/reward programs weighted toward aggressive growth. That category would include small cap companies, high yield bonds, and emerging markets. An aggressive portfolio may be a good choice if the following traits describe you:

- Always looking for high performance

- Can tolerate major price fluctuations

- Are a younger or a more experienced investor

- Have other assets focused on growth and income

Invest for Income

No matter how you drive or invest, as you reach your target retirement age, it's important that your savings and investments be designed to produce monthly income for the rest of your life. Too many Americans approaching retirement have their money in the wrong programs. The family plan begins to fail because of inadequate monthly income or a return of principal.

Remember that stamp collections just like gold, silver, coin collections, artwork, vintage cars, guns, old records, emus, Beanie Babies, Cabbage Patch dolls, baseball cards, and other misguided fads cannot provide monthly income. I know that people who have put their hard-earned money in these fads will disagree with me, and to those people this advice will fall on deaf ears.

THE TWO ENEMIES OF MONEY

Understanding the two enemies of money—inflation and taxes—is essential to your financial future. We can't control inflation, but we can develop and maintain a family financial plan designed to address it. This approach should include long-term investments that are designed to provide both growth and income that meet or exceed the traditional annual inflation rates of 3% to 3½%.

If you want to control taxes, consider tax-free or tax-deferred programs. Hundreds of such vehicles are available. I am always amused to see the net worth statements of those blessed with millions or billions of dollars. Much of it is invested in tax-free and tax-deferred programs. Their advisors are working overtime to minimize taxes.

If you have tax-deferred or tax-free 401(k), Roth 401(k), 403(b), or 457 plans provided by your employer, become familiar with the investment options and retirement payouts. Each dollar invested in a traditional 401(k), 403(b), or 457 reduces your annual taxable income and, therefore, saves you tax dollars each year. By using these employer-sponsored plans to contribute to your future retirement, you reduce your current tax liability by converting taxable income into future retirement income. What a wonderful concept!

INVESTING IN BEAR MARKETS

So why does investing in down markets sound crazy? Consider this. When you go to the store and discover a sale, do you say to yourself, "No, this isn't for me, I'll wait until prices go back up before I buy." Or do you buy as much as you can realistically afford and use? We all know the answer.

There is an old saying in the investment community: "When the stock market goes down, stocks go back to their rightful owners." And that really is smart! Are you going to be part of the success story?

In the bear market of 2000, 2001, and 2002, many workers reduced or stopped contributing to their 401(k) or similar plans. The reason is that when these employees got their quarterly investment statement, they noticed the total value of their account had gone down. Thinking that investing should only happen when the markets are going up, they stopped contributing altogether. What did the smart ones do? They did just the opposite. They increased their investment level to the maximum because they understood the long-term benefits of buying low. They understood the advantage of getting in when the values were down. And years later, in retirement, when they need the money, the investments should be worth substantially more. From 2002 through 2007, the stock market produced huge gains for long-term investors.

Investing in a retirement plan such as a 401(k), 403(b), or 457 is always a win-win situation. I can't repeat this enough—if your employer offers any of these retirement plans, then by all means, participate. How much should you invest? If you can afford it, the maximum allowed by the plan. Why don't more people participate at that level? I believe it's because they don't clearly understand the long-term benefits. At retirement time, they will.

Be sure you're making the
"Right Choices."

10

Reduce Risk by Properly Allocating Assets

Things are not really lost; they're just in a place where they don't belong. Have you lost performance with your money? Is your money where it doesn't belong?

Proper asset allocation involves dividing an investment portfolio among different classes to achieve specific performance goals. At least annually, you should review how much of your assets you have in each category to ensure that the prescribed amounts remain at the stated percentages. To decide the specific allocations, you must understand each category's underlying capability for long-term performance.

As you review your portfolio, are your assets lumped into only one type of savings plan or investment, or are you properly spread among many? The big questions are whether you are properly allocating your assets for long-term performance and if the investment program is working for you.

To be fair and balanced, I point out that asset allocation alone does not guarantee performance. Many investors don't understand what asset allocation really means. Your portfolio's total return depends on how you allocate the investments among selected, long-term vehicles. If you're interested in growth, income, and guarantees, consider some of the new living benefits in annuities.

Now let's take a look at the most common asset categories.

Cash and cash equivalents, such as passbook deposits, CDs, treasury bills, money market accounts, and money market funds, are considered the safest savings programs, but they usually produce the lowest returns. Over the years, people who had thousands sitting idle in checking and savings accounts didn't know why the money was there. I'll tell you the reason. It's out of habit, and to address short-term emergencies. Do you have too much of your money in those accounts? Think back over your lifetime. How many emergencies have required that money to be there? With the advent of credit cards to handle any emergency, the genuine need for idle cash sitting in these accounts has almost disappeared

Stocks, also referred to as *equities*, have historically provided the greatest risk/reward performance among the major asset categories. However, because they are volatile, stocks can be very risky in the short term. Even large company stocks can lose their value. Do the names Enron and WorldCom sound familiar? For the average American, stock picking can be dicey.

Bonds are generally less volatile than stocks but offer more modest returns. As you approach retirement, consider increasing your bond holdings relative to your stock holdings. This tradeoff reduces risk and still offers modest long-term growth. Keep in mind that certain categories of bonds, known as high-yield or "junk" bonds, offer high returns but also carry higher risk/reward ratios.

Collectibles are not an asset class in a formal sense, yet many investors treat them as such. A collectible is any physical asset that is expected to appreciate in value over time. For the average investor, the only thing more harmful to your financial security than too much cash in the bank is having lots of money sunk into collectibles. Putting your hard-earned money in any kind of collectibles is a bad idea, and it certainly should not be a big part of your asset allocation approach.

At one of the radio stations I broadcast from, there was a fellow who collected guitars. After one of my shows, I remember talking with him about buying another guitar. He already owned more than twenty, but like many avid collectors, he didn't understand when enough was enough. I teased him about buying so many guitars. He looked me in the eye and said his guitars were going to represent a major source of retirement income. I wonder how much retirement income he will get from each guitar. From my prospective he's wrong, but it was a difficult task to convince him of that.

There is a strong tendency for some investors to think that the more money they accumulate, the more diversification they need. It's not necessarily true. If you have been successful for years with a certain asset mix, why change your approach? During this period, you have accumulated wealth, minimized taxes, and reached or exceeded your performance goals. Your family financial plan has simplified your tax return; deferred taxes on the interest, gains, and dividends you are not using; and created ways to pass wealth to your beneficiaries outside of probate. If you have all this covered, then don't change what's working. If you don't have it together, now is the time to start.

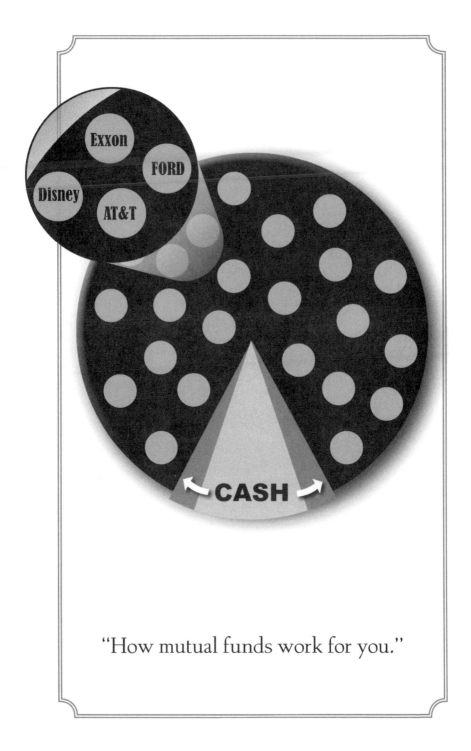

"How mutual funds work for you."

11

What Does a Mutual Fund Look Like?

Looks can be deceiving.

Starting in the 1920s, most Americans were interested, while not actively involved, in mutual funds; but the growth in employer-sponsored payroll retirement plans dramatically heightened all of that. Most of the plans offered mutual funds as investment options, and the associated terminology became household words. Unfortunately, many employees to this day have not done well with these types of programs due to a basic lack of understanding.

During my first year on the radio in 1984, a woman called to ask about mutual funds. She wanted to know how they worked, what's in a mutual fund, how much do they earn, and is the income taxable. Then she asked me, "What does a mutual fund look like?" I had never answered that question before, but it was a great way to help her to become familiar with the benefits of mutual funds.

There are many different types of funds, but this is what a large cap stock mutual fund looks like. Draw a circle and put a bunch of dots inside. Label each dot with a different company name—Boeing, Disney, Exxon-Mobil, GM, IBM,

McDonald's, Microsoft, and any other major companies you are familiar with. Now you have the ingredients of an equity mutual fund: many stocks owned by various investors for the stated purpose of long-term growth and income.

The Start of Mutual Funds

In 1924, a group of Boston businessmen came up with a novel way of investing in the stock market. They organized the first mutual fund, which they called a trust. It was designed as a public offering to attract investors to purchase shares in a diversified portfolio of blue chip companies. They called it the Massachusetts Investors Trust, and it is now considered the very first mutual fund.

The fund consisted solely of blue chip stocks. The phrase "blue chip" came from the game of poker, where the most valuable playing chip is blue. On Wall Street, the term "blue chip" refers to stock of nationally recognized, well-established, and financially sound companies. The Massachusetts Investors Trust included companies such as General Electric that were widely recognized for their products or services. Today its top holdings include JPMorgan Chase, Johnson & Johnson, United Technologies Corporation, and Cisco Systems Inc.

Mutual funds were designed to handle greater market fluctuations than individual stocks. They did just that as they weathered the Stock Market Crash of 1929, the Great Depression, World War II, the Korean and Vietnam Wars, the invasion of Iraq, the assassination of a president, the resignation of a president, the impeachment of a president, the increase in the price of crude oil from $3 per barrel to more than $100 per barrel, double-digit inflation in the 1970s, and, sadly, the introduction of terrorism to American shores in 2001.

As of 2007, Boomers comprise nearly 20% of the adult population. This large population group looked for new ways to invest for retirement and turned its sights on the mutual fund industry. As Boomers invested billions into mutual funds, mutual fund companies expanded their offerings to include corporate bonds, treasuries, municipal bonds, small cap companies, mid cap companies, and foreign companies. Today many of the large mutual funds have millions of investors and billions of dollars under management.

Unlike with individual stocks, you don't buy a mutual fund; you invest in a mutual fund. The funds are offered by a prospectus, a document in which the investment company describes the types of securities that the investment contains. The prospectus also outlines the goal of the fund, which is typically one of three objectives: growth, growth and income, or income. Each mutual fund offers different opportunities to investors, and each comes with different risk/reward goals and objectives. Mutual funds are used by religious organizations, foundations, trusts, universities, pension plans, 401(k)s, 403(b)s, 457s, profit-sharing plans, and individuals through IRAs and ROTH-IRAs.

Mutual Funds 101

Mutual funds are typically expressed as three numbers: the number of shares you own, the share price, and your account value. Multiply the number of shares you own by the current share price and you arrive at the current account total value. The share price doesn't fluctuate throughout the day, and it is always expressed as of the prior day's closing price. If you purchase or liquidate shares, regardless of the time of day that you place the order, the transaction is executed at the day's closing price.

Some mutual funds declare dividends and capital gains throughout the year. When that happens, the mutual fund management adds more shares to the account relative to the dividend or capital gain payout, but the value of the shares is reduced so that the total value change is zero as a result of the gain (or dividend declaration).

Past performance of mutual funds does not guarantee future results. We've all heard the disclosure many times. The statement is true, but it needs to be further examined. There is no guarantee that your value in the fund will go up or down. However, logic says that if a fund has performed consistently for years, maybe decades, it's highly probable that the fund will continue to perform consistently over time. Long-term trends can help us decide where, when, or how to invest in a mutual fund.

Long-term investors seek performance with an acceptable level of risk. They don't look for a mutual fund with a history of poor performance. If a fund has performed poorly for an extended period, few informed investors are excited about putting their money at that level of risk. Long-term low performance drives investors away. In fact, the flow of money away from a mutual fund with poor performance is the best type of empirical evidence you can find. If poor results have been long-term, the fund may close or be acquired by another investment company, which may result in additional expenses and further losses to investors. Mutual funds disclose performance on a one-, three-, five-, and ten-year basis. Performance is expressed net of expenses.

Many mutual fund companies offer a variety of share classes to investors. Each share class carries a different pricing structure, which is explained in the prospectus. As an investor, you should know how the specific fund is organized to be able to decide if it is the right one to assist in achieving your goals.

You should know that mutual fund companies are prohibited from giving any financial advice. When you call to ask for information or to place a purchase or liquidate order, the voice on the other end of the phone is an order taker, not an advisor. They place transactions that presumably have been carefully analyzed by an educated investor and their advisor.

Mutual Funds Are Highly Regulated

Mutual funds are considered one of the most regulated investments programs available to the public. They are regulated by the Securities and Exchange Commission (SEC). The SEC's function is to review the proposed prospectus before its distribution to the public.

As of July 2007, mutual funds and other financial investment companies also receive oversight by the Financial Industry
Regulatory Authority (FINRA). FINRA is the largest regula-
tor for all securities firms doing business with the public. It
oversees nearly 5,100 brokerage firms, about 173,000 branch
offices, and more than 665,000 registered securities represen-
tatives. FINRA was created by consolidating the National
Association of Securities Dealers (NASD) and the member
regulation, enforcement, and arbitration functions of the New
York Stock Exchange.

BE AWARE OF NEW PARADIGMS FOR INVESTING

In the bull market of the 1980s and 1990s, the stock market—and particularly the large capitalized companies—enjoyed
substantial price growth. If you had invested in large cap companies through mutual funds such as the Standard & Poor's
(S&P) 500, then your local journalist would have to do little
homework to report how well those types of funds performed.
From my travels throughout the country in the '90s, it seemed
that financial journalists were reading each other's articles and
therefore arriving at the same erroneous conclusion: that the
S&P 500 index mutual funds were the best investment in the
country. You probably read the same thing.

Index funds are passively managed, meaning that the fund
manager precisely tracks the S&P 500 selections by holding the same percentage of stocks as those held in the S&P
portfolio. Other funds are actively managed, meaning that the

fund manager buys and sells stocks and bonds to reposition their portfolios relative to changing market conditions. As a result, actively managed mutual funds performed differently than the S&P 500 over various time frames.

Financial journalists during this period neglected to do their homework. They wrote in their articles that the S&P beat most of managed funds. If most of managed funds did worse than the S&P 500, then by definition, some did better. Aren't you curious about the names of the funds that beat the S&P index funds? Why didn't journalists investigate and advise readers about the top performing funds?

The S&P 500—A Benchmark

Since the S&P 500 is a benchmark, mutual fund investors in these types of index funds learned that the index could become heavily weighted in technology and internet stocks, and suffer substantial losses as it did by March 2000. Then the big bear appeared, and the sky-high price-to-earnings ratio stocks lost more than 45% by October 2002.

So how does the S&P 500 Index select U.S. companies to be included in the group? A committee at Standard & Poor's reviews the stock holdings each year and, according to internal criteria, may change the stock selections in the index. If the S&P committee wants more growth, the result is less dividends paid, because growth stocks generally don't pay dividends. A common complaint about the S&P 500 mutual funds is the low dividend payout of around 1.5%.

When the financial TV stations broadcast a "Man in the Street" story, most of those interviewed have no idea of the makeup of the S&P 500, although many acknowledge putting money into that type of mutual fund through their company 401(k) plan. They openly admit to all viewers they have no idea what they are doing. Wow!

Investors are surprised to learn there aren't equal amounts of company stock in the S&P 500 Index. S&P uses a formula to weight one stock over another in deciding how many shares to buy of each stock. This approach is called "capitalization weighting." If the weighting is higher in low-dividend-paying stocks, the overall yield of that mutual fund will drop. If the weighting is heavier in dividend-paying stocks, the yield of the mutual fund will increase.

One other point of interest—there are no bonds in the S&P 500 Index, because the fund is made up of 500 U.S. company stocks. As of November 1, 2004, an investment of $100,000 in an S&P 500 Index in 1999 remained in a negative position, having lost thousands depending on when one invested. If an investor were withdrawing income at a rate of 5% per year, the mutual fund's total value dropped another 25% over the five-year period, and the original withdrawal amounts would be too high to be sustained over a ten- to twenty-year period. A scenario like this could clearly destroy a long-term plan.

"It's GUARANTEED!"

12

If You Want Guarantees, Consider Tax-Deferred Annuities

A variable annuity looks like a Thanksgiving pie cut in pieces, with each slice representing an investment selection. A fixed annuity looks like a pie that hasn't been cut.

In 1988, an elderly woman came to my office accompanied by her CPA. The CPA had listened to my radio program for several months, later attended one of my seminars, and recommended a fixed annuity for her client, Dorothy. According to the CPA, she had millions sitting in several Dallas savings and loans and wanted to reposition those accounts because she believed many of them had been taken over by a shady bunch of characters robbing the banks blind. As it turned out, she was right.

Initially, Dorothy placed $2.8 million in an annuity. During our conversation, I asked about beneficiaries, and her story got interesting. Her husband had died thirty years before, and she had never remarried. She had no children, so her siblings and other relatives would ultimately get all her money. The problem was that Dorothy felt her relatives didn't appreciate her or what she had accomplished with her money.

As an example, she told me about her annual $10,000 Christmas gift to each member of the family. For years, what began as a seasonal gesture had since evolved into an expected tradition. On December 15, family members would arrive at her home, drop off a poinsettia or other small gift, and march over to the table that held the marked envelopes with the names in bold print and the checks inside. The stack was an inch high. Family members would quickly sort through the stack until they found their envelope and then quietly walk out the door.

Her generosity had evolved into quick visits to pick up the check without even a cordial "thank you" to this kind woman. Dorothy became deeply disappointed and naturally felt unappreciated for her annual gifts. She asked me if I had any ideas.

As an outsider observing the family dynamics, I told her not to sign the checks. This would immediately stop the family from treating her this way. When the relatives called to ask about the missing signature, she could tell them to bring the family for a visit to share more about their busy lives. Dorothy's family changed their habits immediately, many apologizing for their past behavior.

And now for the bizarre stuff.

Some time later, I received a phone call from Dorothy's brother advising me that Dorothy had suddenly died. Since he was one of the primary beneficiaries, I advised him to forward a death certificate to my office, as required by the annuity company before we could process the death claim. He became irritated and said I didn't need any such certificate. He wanted the claim processed immediately, with the checks issued to the family members within a week. He further indicated that if I failed to respond to the claim he would turn his attorney loose on me. When I asked how she died, he mumbled something about it being too complicated to describe.

His behavior was so strange that I became suspicious. Then I recalled Dorothy telling me that her brother and sister-in-law were always asking her for money, and no matter how much she gave, it was never enough.

Dorothy lived with her sister, so I called the sister to get the details surrounding this tragic event. But it wasn't her sister who answered the phone. You guessed it. It was Dorothy. I told her about the brother's phone call and, of course, she wasn't surprised. She told me that he had also called several of her banks trying the same scam. Lovely family.

Annuities Are Unique Because of Their Guarantees

Most Americans seem to be somewhat familiar with the term "annuity" but at the same time find it difficult to explain how annuities actually work. The essence of an annuity is that it offers certain stipulated guarantees.

An annuity is a contract issued by a reserve life insurance company. It is generally a tax-deferred savings or investment program that can provide income through systematic withdrawals or, upon annuitization, make regular payments to an annuitant for a certain period. The payments can be structured for one or more individual's lifetimes. It may also include a death benefit that will pay your beneficiary a guaranteed minimum amount, such as your total purchase payment less withdrawals and/or a living benefit that guarantees income for life.

If you consider an annuity, ask about the various guarantees for your money. The guarantees are only as strong as the claims-paying ability of the issuing company. Seek out the help of an experienced advisor when you consider these programs.

Annuities may have higher expenses than mutual funds, but mutual funds do not provide guarantees. What a great country, to have so many opportunities to make money!

TYPES OF ANNUITIES

Generally, there are three types of annuities: immediate, fixed, and variable.

With an *immediate annuity*, you agree to issue a check, called a premium, to the insurance company; in return, the company stipulates that it will make monthly, quarterly, or annual payments to the annuitant (you) for a certain period. The payout period is stipulated at the time of issuance of the contract. For example, it may be structured for a period of five years or as long as your entire lifetime.

Annuities have several uses. For instance, many corporate pension plans use immediate annuities to pay retirees monthly income for life. In lawsuits, the judge may award a structured settlement for losses and specify the use of an immediate annuity to pay the claims.

Fixed annuities guarantee a fixed rate of interest for a fixed period of time, hence the name "fixed." This type of annuity is very popular with conservative savers. Usually, the longer the contract period, the higher the fixed interest rate paid to the annuitant. In this type of vehicle, you do not select how the money will be invested by the insurance company.

In most states, fixed annuities are guaranteed up to a certain level by a formula developed within the office of the state insurance commissioner, which is supported annually by a portion of the taxes or premiums related to the insurance companies doing business in that state.

Variable annuities require the owner to choose how the money is invested from a range of different options known as sub-accounts. Variable annuities have been available for over fifty years. The benefit of a variable annuity is that owners can participate in the tax-deferred benefits of a rising stock market, while their beneficiaries are protected from losing their original investment if the owner dies.

Variable annuity beneficiaries who lost their spouse in 2000, 2001, and 2002 didn't also lose their principal, because the money was guaranteed as part of the benefits of the contract. Most beneficiaries simply could not believe they were going to receive a stepped-up amount as a result of the annuity death benefit. That is why so many retirees elect to rollover their 401ks and pension plans into variable annuities. This type of investment enables the owner to participate in the financial markets with a guaranteed death benefit. As always, do the research with your advisor to get the right annuity for you and your family.

I have encountered husbands who don't want to pay the additional expense for the guarantees—and therefore give up the death benefits—while the wife wants all the long-term financial security she can get. These conversations can get rather chilly when a husband even implies that his wife isn't worth the additional costs. My office chair is on rollers, and when we get to this point, I usually move back from the table and let the discussion unfold before I comment. (I'd like to be a fly on the ceiling of their car as this conversation continues on the ride back home. Envision the emotions as the wife asks, "What do you mean, I'm not worth it?")

When it's my turn to comment, I talk about the guaranteed death benefits and the guaranteed living benefits of annuities versus mutual funds, the performance of each, and the related expenses, and I let my clients make the final decision. I do not recommend one over the other, because it's really up to the individual to consider the cost/benefit relationship in order to make an informed decision. Some investors even choose to divide the investments equally between mutual funds and a variable annuity.

My experience is that when women are in charge of the final decision, to a person, they choose the variable annuity based on the long-term performance track record they see in the prospectus and the death benefits they can pass on to their husbands. Many men, however, thinking they will die first, often look the other way relative to the guaranteed death benefit and choose mutual funds.

Another benefit of annuities is that when the owner dies, the proceeds in the annuity pass outside of probate. That can be important, because it means this part of the family wealth passes to beneficiaries in private without the delays and disclosures required by the probate court system. Most people want to transfer family wealth in private, and an annuity can ensure it happens that way.

A few states also extend asset protection to annuity contracts, which means annuities are protected from creditors and bankruptcies. In my home state of Texas, annuities are protected. If an attorney is preparing to file a suit on behalf of a client against you and, during the discovery process, finds that the majority of your assets are in annuities, the attorney typically drops the case. Those who are self employed, or have sizeable amounts of cash, owners of businesses, and others who have accumulated wealth and want to protect their family assets often choose annuities for this very reason. Because so many Americans are getting smarter with their money, each year billions are placed in annuities for the purpose of building tax deferred wealth, planning their estates, deferring current taxes, and in some states like Texas, protecting assets from lawsuits.

INDEX ANNUITIES

Index annuities are a form of a fixed annuity. These are complicated savings vehicles, so complicated that I have never met anyone who can completely explain how they work, including the insurance agents who offer them. Index annuities pay a fixed interest rate, usually 3%. That fits them into a savings program, not an investment program. Because index annuities are considered savings programs, many states don't require a securities license to offer them to the public.

In general, index annuities offer a combination of the greater of a fixed-interest rate or a percentage-participation interest rate, as calculated by the performance of an index. The participation rate can have a monthly or annual cap established by each annuity company. If the participation percentage is 30%, which is common, and the index is the S&P 500, which has realized an 8% gain for the year, the owner of the index annuity receives a participation interest at the rate of 30% of the 8%, or 2.4%. If the fixed interest rate was 3%, the owner would receive the higher rate, or 3% that year. If the participation rate was 40% and the index achieved an 8% increase, the index annuity participation would be 3.2%. Not much risk for an insurance company, is there?

Are index annuities right for you? As in any other important financial decision, get a clear understanding of the terms, and then call the insurance company offering the annuity to ask exactly what the actual interest was during the prior years, AND get it in writing. Also ask about the long holding periods with substantial penalties.

QUALIFIED AND NON-QUALIFIED

Annuities are further classified as qualified or non-qualified, according to the way the account is initially funded. This distinction affects the tax treatment of the distributions to the annuitant.

Qualified annuities are generally funded from pension and

retirement plans that have not been taxed and remain untaxed until the distributions are paid to the annuitant. Qualified annuity programs can include defined benefit pension plans, profit sharing plans, 401(k), 403(b), 457, IRA rollovers and transfers. Generally, the distributions from qualified annuities, known as required mandatory distributions, must start in the year that the owner reaches age 70½.

Non-qualified Annuities are funded by money previously taxed. The earnings are permitted to grow tax-deferred, until the distribution is paid to the annuitant. Depending on the structure of the payout process, the distributions could be partially taxable or 100% taxable. According to the tax code, earnings are typically distributed first, a tax approach commonly known as LIFO, or last-in-first-out. The last monies coming into the annuity are earnings, and they are taxed as ordinary income when withdrawn.

"It's tax deferred until
withdrawals are made."

13

Reduce Your Taxes with a 401(k)

Each year Americans spend more
time planning their vacations than
planning for their retirement.

As worldwide competition for goods and services increased
in the late 1970s and 1980s, profit margins for many American
companies began to shrink. At the same time, CEOs and other
high-level managers received huge bonuses. To balance the
books, many large corporations stopped funding traditional
defined-benefit pension plans.

Simultaneously, in the early 1980s, the 401(k) plan
emerged as a replacement for the defined-benefit pension plan.
As a result, funding and management of retirement accounts
shifted from the employer directly to the employee. This was a
dramatic change from the past, and as I have discussed many
times on our radio and TV programs, it may be the worst thing
that ever happened to employees.

The 401(k) plan is a type of employer-sponsored, defined-
contribution retirement plan named after the 401(k) section
of the U.S. Internal Revenue Code. The code reference also
explains why other employer-sponsored plans are known as
403(b) or 457 plans. Eventually, as the Internal Revenue Code
is modified, all of these plans will have similar characteristics.

A 401(k) plan allows a worker to save for retirement while deferring income taxes on the investment's earnings until withdrawals are made. The 401(k) permits the employee to fund the program through payroll contributions on a tax-deductible basis, which reduces annual taxable income dollar for dollar. That's very attractive for all employees. In fact, in the early days of the 401(k), reducing taxes was the primary reason offered by most employees who contributed part of their paycheck into the plan. Many corporations offer employee matching amounts up to a specified maximum level, usually 6%.

Despite its many advantages, the 401(k) system has failed for many workers. The company 401(k) plan is designed so that the employee determines what amount, if any, will be invested each month. Only then will the company contribute to the plan. That's how it works—if you don't contribute, neither will your employer. So if the employee fails to contribute, the company puts nothing into the plan. The thinking behind the 401(k) is that employees are completely responsible for making their own investment and retirement decisions. Surveys tell us that without formal training in how investments work, most employees have a deep fear about making these kinds of financial decisions. However, if you invest correctly in your 401(k), it should be the largest retirement asset you own.

In the early 1980s, many 401(k) employers were confused about the number of investment selections available within each plan, and employers had restrictions on the kinds of advice they could provide to a financially illiterate workforce. To limit expenses and confusion, many companies offered only one to three investment choices. As more information became available from the investment community, companies realized they should broaden the number and types of investment selections offered within the plan. The new approach heightened the use of the 401(k) plans, and today most companies who want to attract and maintain a dedicated work force offer some form of 401(k) plan.

Although corporate America had the ability to counsel employees about investing, the liabilities associated with giving such financial advice were considered too high. As a result, today's employees with no investment training are forced to make their own decisions that directly affect their life in retirement. Most employees acknowledge they receive their 401(k) investment advice from co-workers who also are untrained in the actual risk/reward features of the various investment selections. Sounds like the blind leading the blind and hoping someone has a sense of direction. Most don't.

What to Do with Multiple 401(k) Plans from Former Employers

According to the Department of Labor Statistics, American workers change jobs every four years. As a result, employees are subjected to a new group of 401(k) investment selections with each job change. Managing more than one 401(k) plan can become a major problem, and it's the reason most often given for not participating in the new company's retirement plan.

For purposes of simplification, you might consider rolling over several smaller plans into a stretch IRA in order to manage a single account. Making this choice also offers an opportunity to seek the help of a financial advisor who can provide professional recommendations to you. To affect a roll-over at some companies, you still need to contact the human resource (HR) department of your former employer to get the necessary paperwork to make the change. Then contact your financial advisor who can guide you as to how to handle the rollover without taxes.

"I made the Right Choices; have you?"

14

And Now the IRAs

Retirement seemed a long way off . . . but so did turning 50.

The individual retirement account (IRA) has been around for a long time, but the 1981 Economic Recovery Tax Act (ERTA), promoted by President Ronald Reagan, took the IRA to a new level. According to ERTA, a worker with a salary of at least $2,000 could put up to $2,000 per year in to the traditional IRA and deduct that amount from his or her taxable income. Doing so converts tax dollars into future retirement income. Now that is a sterling idea!

Many who have IRAs, or are considering an IRA, refer to these accounts as an investment. That is not technically correct, because an IRA is a financial vehicle in which you can place savings or investments. When I explain an IRA, I typically draw an empty circle and write the name of the owner with IRA next to their name on top of the circle. Inside the circle, I list the types of investments that can be placed in an IRA. Almost any savings or investment imaginable can be placed inside of the circle. When you think of an IRA, envision an empty circle and then fill in your choice of investments relative to your long-term retirement goals.

The annual contribution to an IRA is treated as a deduction on your tax return under the section "Adjustments to Income." The account is considered a "qualified" program because the contribution and the earnings qualify for special tax treatment. According to ERTA of 1981, the non-working spouse could also have a $250 account each year. With a creative allocation, there could be an even split with the $2,250 total amount between the two spouses.

Unfortunately, in the beginning many workers contributed to an IRA each year primarily to save taxes, without understanding that the main reason for IRAs was to build wealth for retirement income. Realizing that our savings level in America was falling behind, President Reagan encouraged Congress to add the tax-saving feature as an incentive to motivate Americans to put money away for retirement. And it worked. Under ERTA, all workers, regardless of their income level, were eligible to contribute to a traditional IRA.

Sadly, that changed in 1986. From my perspective, Ronald Reagan was not thinking clearly when he signed the new tax bill into law that eliminated certain salary levels from being eligible for tax-deductible contributions. Why would it be such a great idea for all workers in 1981 and a bad idea for certain income levels in 1986?

IRA tax law has changed many times. Most notably, the IRA maximum tax-deductible contribution amount has increased. In 2007, the maximum tax-deductible amount was $4,000 per working person. Those over age 50 had a catch-up provision that permitted an annual tax-deductible contribution of $5,000. For two spouses over age 50, $10,000 per year is a lot to invest for retirement. In future years, the contribution will be indexed, which means that the annual maximum contribution will increase relative to a government cost-of-living formula and salary threshold.

IRA ROLLOVERS

Few employees work for the same company their entire working life and enter retirement with a monthly pension funded 100% by one company. Today, most of us reach retirement having had several jobs and employers. Prior to 1986, as employees moved from one company to another, many withdrew their 401(k) retirement plan checks and spent the money. The withdrawal was treated as 100% taxable, plus employees owed an additional 10% penalty if the person was under age 59½. If the employee did not report the taxable transaction, the IRS pursued them for filing a fraudulent tax return. Back taxes, penalties, and interest were severe.

To reduce the problems associated with these growing tax issues, the Internal Revenue Service asked Congress to change the tax laws. Today companies are required to make forms available to employees who elect an IRA rollover without any tax consequences. And here is the big change. If a former employee decides to take the money and spend it, the former employer must be advised of the employee's intentions in writing, withhold the appropriate income taxes, and report the transaction to the IRS. It took a while to figure it out, but now the system appears to work well for all concerned.

As employees move their various pension plans from their former employers to a rollover IRA, the accounts are liquidated, a check is issued in the name of the new IRA custodian, and the proceeds are rolled over to that account, all tax deferred. The rollover check should not be issued in the name of the employee, or there could be significant tax problems and penalties associated with the transaction.

For tax purposes, when both qualified and nonqualified funds are rolled over from an employer plan to an IRA, each plan must be allocated as qualified or nonqualified in order to avoid double taxation. That information should be filed on IRS Form 8606. The reason for allocating the amounts and filing the information with the IRS is to be able to withdraw a certain percentage of income from the accounts on both a tax-free and a taxable basis simultaneously. That's tax planning.

Once you've set up your rollover IRA, you may make withdrawals from the account immediately. If you aren't aged 59½, a 10% early-withdrawal excise tax penalty may be applied. But there are specific provisions in the tax code under Section 72t that permit penalty-free income withdrawals prior to age 59½. Discuss this in detail with your financial and tax advisor before starting the withdrawals.

Roth IRA

In 1998, another IRA, known as the Roth IRA, was created and named after Senator William Roth from Delaware. The Roth IRA is different from the traditional IRA because the annual contributions for a worker are not tax deductible, but the withdrawals are tax-free if the account is in place for five years and the account holder's age has reached 59½.

Should the contribution portion be withdrawn prior to the two restrictions, it is treated as a tax-free distribution because it is considered a return of the after-tax contributions. If the earnings are also withdrawn without satisfying the two requirements, it is taxed as ordinary income with a 10% penalty. OUCH!

The maximum contribution amounts for a Roth IRA are the same as the traditional IRA, but you can't contribute annually to both of them at their maximum levels. You can, however, prorate different amounts to both traditional IRAs and Roth IRAs in the same year as long as you don't exceed the maximum amount relative to your age. Some folks over age 50 who are entitled to contribute $5,000 per year may contribute $2,500 to the traditional IRA and $2,500 to the Roth IRA the same year. Each program has a financial benefit depending on the individual's tax and income level.

Many in the financial service industry have questioned the potential tax law changes and the income from the Roth IRA becoming taxable? I believe they will. Personally, I think the debt of our country will become so high that all sources of income will be taxed through a "means test."

Remember the Romans.

Stretch IRA

Many associated with the financial services industry deny that a stretch IRA exists. Several years ago, a major tax law change affected the way beneficiaries receive proceeds from an IRA after the death of the account's owner. Before the change, children designated as IRA beneficiaries would receive the entire distribution as a 100% taxable event, paid immediately or over a five-year period. According to tax law at that time, terminating the IRA at the death of the owner was mandatory. In many instances, the distribution amount was so large that the highest federal and state income tax and estate tax brackets were applied, creating sizeable tax problems for the heirs and destroying the account owner's estate planning.

With the tax law change, if the IRA custodian treats it as a stretch IRA, the entire account is passed intact as an IRA to the children or other non-spouse beneficiary without any income tax consequences. That is a huge change. The new beneficiary owner of the inherited IRA is responsible for withdrawing a certain amount each year based on age as determined by an IRS table that is promulgated to the public.

Any IRA can be considered a stretch IRA if the custodian elects to treat it that way. A stretch IRA has nothing to do with required minimum distributions, known as RMDs, or the way the owner withdraws income from the account.

Other Types of IRAs

The IRA concept has been expanded for broader application to corporations and sole proprietors. Some are known as simplified employee pension IRAs, or SEP-IRAs. These are available for individuals who want their company to fund the plan 100% for all employees. They can be used in small corporations or sole proprietorships with minimum employees. The contribution amount changes each year, relative to compensation and new percentage levels provided by the tax code. Your advisor should be able to keep you current on the changes as they happen. Small businesses can also use simple-IRAs, which require that an employee contribute to the plan prior to employer contributions. The annual contribution levels are less than those for SEPs so these types of plans are not popular.

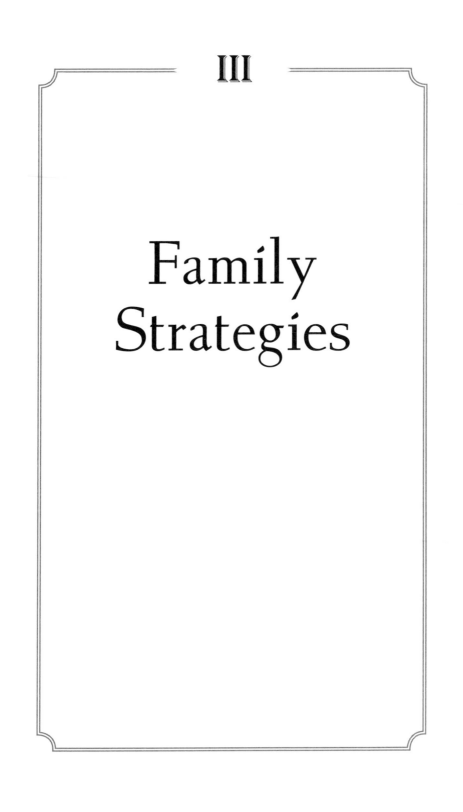

III

Family
Strategies

"It's a family affair."

15

Create a Family Financial Plan

Always carry a happy checkbook.

There are two schools of thought concerning a family financial plan. One says it's not necessary to have a plan in writing; the other says it has to be in writing to have any chance of success.

A written plan identifies the goals, objectives, asset allocation guidelines, selected investment vehicles, estimated performance earnings, and projected value of the investment portfolio. A written plan can be quite simple. The plan should include annual investment updates as a reference tool for measuring the success of the family plan. Whether your plan is written or not, you need a plan, and you need it now.

If you choose to prepare a written plan, list all working assets and a proposed timetable for implementing various parts of the plan. List each goal, when you expect to achieve the goal, what action is necessary for the results you want, when you will start each part of the plan, and where you will invest. Each of these topics should receive equally important consideration. When you determine the amount you need to invest on a monthly basis, start your program immediately.

If all this sounds like too much effort, consider the following sample plan.

Goal: to accumulate $1 million in working assets that produce monthly income at the rate of 5% annually, or $50,000 each year. That amount, combined with Social Security benefits of $25,000, annually produces $75,000 or more each year.

Now that's not complicated, is it?

For purposes of getting started, consider investing 5% to10% of your take-home pay each month. If that is too much, start at a lower amount and increase the monthly percentage with each salary change while eliminating credit card and car/truck debt. As strange as this may seem, I really want you to form the habit of regular monthly investing. The amount invested isn't critical in the beginning. What is important is forming a new, positive habit of investing. And it is essential that you get started right away.

When you are ready to choose an investment, I suggest starting with a mutual fund. There are thousands to choose from. For young investors, aged 20 to 50, I typically place a strong emphasis on growth funds. Growth funds are designed to provide long-term dynamic growth in the small-to mid-cap and emerging market categories. Growth funds are among the most aggressive types of funds, which means they have the potential to gain or lose in value.

Investors aged 50 and older may consider a less aggressive fund that focuses on growth and income. Now here is an important point. If the accounts are designed to be passed on to the family, factor in the ages of the intended beneficiaries and invest according to their ages when you consider risk and reward.

For investors 60 and older, and particularly those already enjoying retirement, I have a lot of confidence in specifically selected, balanced funds. These funds are typically 50% to 65% stocks, with the remaining portion in bonds and money-market accounts. Not all balanced funds perform in the same manner, but the ones we are interested in perform like the traditional defined-benefit pension plans. They are more predictable because the fund managers are continuously rebalancing the stock-to-bond ratio in order to maintain the designed allocation. During the bear market of 2000–2002, balanced funds generally performed differently than the growth funds. Discuss them with your advisor.

Create the Habit of Investing

We all have habits formed over time. For those of us who are working, we usually get up at a certain time, eat the same breakfast, drive the same roads, park in the same area, walk into the same office, and greet the same people. We are creatures of habit, and if we have formed good habits, our lives should be peaceful and rewarding. I would like you to form the habit of monthly investing for your financial security. If this wonderful but simple concept of monthly investing spreads across the country, we could change the way America thinks about money, and our debt at all levels would slowly disappear.

A strange thing happens as your investment statements arrive in the mail. You get excited watching your account grow as you fulfill your family plan. What a great feeling! Think of being the first in your family to enjoy a comfortable retirement. You will walk with confidence, knowing that something very special is happening.

Now you ask, "Where does the money come from to invest in these plans?" When you invest through your employer-sponsored program, the amount invested is deducted from your paycheck. Each dollar invested reduces your taxable income, dollar for dollar, thereby providing the additional money for the investment plan. Many employees, due to high personal debt, start with a 1% payroll deduction. Each time they receive a salary increase, they increase the percentage, until they attain a level that can be properly sustained. When considering how much to invest, don't focus on the minimum amount, think about the maximum for a better retirement.

Another powerful aspect of your family financial plan will be to reduce or stop misusing credit cards. That includes the daily $3.50 latte, the $5.00 pack of cigarettes, the $5.00 beer, the $1.00 bottle of water, the twice monthly $25.00 manicures, the $1.00 vending machine snacks, the unused gym membership at $35.00 per month, and, of course, the daily $2.50 of interest due on the credit cards. That totals more than $6,000 per year, and I didn't include your weekly fill-up of gas. I suggest you perform plastic surgery on the credit cards by cutting them in half. But don't cancel them, because cards with zero balances improve your credit rating. Keep one or two, at the most, active. Even your wallet will be reduced in size.

Economics dictate that we attack the credit card with the highest rate of interest. How do you know which ones charge the most? Call them. Then immediately develop a family plan to reduce that specific debt first. Don't look back, and don't let any member of your family, friends, or co-workers discourage you from creating positive habits. Remember, habits change our lives.

Points to Consider

Your family financial plan is all about spending less than you make, paying off outstanding debt, getting rid of unnecessary credit cards, and investing a portion of your take-home pay each month. It's that simple. You now have a sound family financial plan for the rest of your life. Just stop talking about it and do it.

"Help your parents;
some day it will be your turn."

16

Discuss Finances with Your Aging Parents

The memories of a lifetime are priceless; for everything else there is financial planning.

An elderly gentlemen and his wife once told me the reason they didn't prepare for retirement was because they believed it was their children's responsibility to take care of them, just as children had done in the old country. This couple had four children and expected to spend three months every year with each child. What a shock to the family! When I asked them where they were going to live the second year, the question startled them.

Money is a very sensitive subject to discuss with your parents. Many families don't discuss finances. They just flat-out don't. Why? Because it's a complicated and intimidating subject. What parents are willing to admit to their children that they never knew what they were doing when it came to investing? Many parents would rather pretend they are knowl-edgeable than admit the truth. Deep inside, they feel that others their own age are much smarter about money than they are. Somehow these "other people" are wealthier and wiser and debt free. And, of course, their families are enjoying a bet-ter life. It's not true, of course. Most families are in the same financial predicament, because they have no formal training in analyzing investments.

Money comes to us without instructions. Most of us know how to earn a living, and some of us are recognized as specialists in our chosen profession. But even experts in industry, although they won't admit it, are often uneducated about the intricacies of investing. To make matters worse, many in America are afraid of investing. The older generation of Americans—those who came through the Great Depression—have a deep fear about putting their money anywhere out of reach. They constantly worry about finances. Tragically, this group often becomes a financial burden to their family due to poor performance of their assets.

Many older folks who are intimidated by Wall Street avoid investing, and they unfortunately encourage others to do the same. "Be careful with your money, because you never know," they say, meaning, I suppose that keeping your nest egg under a mattress where you can get to it is somehow wiser than investing for long-term growth, as long as your house does not burn down.

In the absence of financial guidance, many aged parents fall prey to shady marketing schemes because their thinking capacity may be limited. The scam artists who descend upon a city or town know this as they set up boiler shops in cheap motels and use unscrupulous salespeople to target retirees. These con artists place calls at specific times of the day to attract the highest numbers of vulnerable people. Their only objective is to separate the older folks from their hard-earned money and direct it into Ponzi scams that can ruin a family financially.

Examples include paying a premium for nonexistent gold and silver coins, fake stock options, and commodity futures that promise outrageous returns. Sadly, many older parents also become willing participants in telemarketing schemes because they want someone to talk to.

Where Are the Records?

As our parents age, it makes sense to ask about family records, life insurance documents, medical insurance plans, and investment portfolios. Adult children should always know where important documents are located. They should be able to quickly locate wills, real estate deeds, mortgages, powers of attorney, credit cards and related revolving-credit statements, and a list of assets, including mutual funds, IRA statements, annuities, Social Security benefits, pension income, bank statements, and CDs.

These discussions can be especially difficult because a parent's dignity may be easily bruised. As our parents age, the next generation becomes the new protectors of the family assets. It's really important that we talk to our parents to help them address the financial status of the family. When we prepare for these discussions, it's wise to start with some general questions.

- Do the parents have enough income to maintain their current lifestyle?

- What are the sources of income?

- How will they pay for medical care?

- Can they afford assisted living or nursing home care?

These extremely important issues must be discussed while your parents have their faculties and before they get sick and emotions run high. Most adult children find it awkward to discuss money matters with parents. And many parents find it awkward to discuss money matters with their children. The reason is simple: traditionally, parents are used to giving advice, not receiving it. For your parents to admit that all these years they had little idea what they were doing with their money can be very painful. If your parents initially resist your questions, continue to press on in a gentle, loving way. Point out that you want to help them make informed decisions to protect their assets. Center the discussions on their security.

These parent/child discussions should be a collective affair. Involve all your siblings to avoid any suspicions that you or others are trying to corner the inheritance or might misguide your parents into making bad decisions. Begin by making reference to a relative or friend who had a recent heart attack, stroke, or other life-threatening illness. Ask your parents how prepared that person's family was to respond to the medical crisis. Then raise the question about how they think your family could handle the same problem.

No one wants to admit to getting old. No one! So place a high priority on listening. Don't overwhelm your parents with too many questions at once. They may not respond in the manner in which you expected. Your parents may take the comments and think on them for days, weeks, or even months before they offer a reasonable explanation of the finances to the family. Try to make it clear that you want to help your parents approach a difficult time in their lives. Do this in a loving way. Some day it will be your turn.

"The ultimate financial plan for college."

17

529 Education Plans

Winning requires the ability to be prepared.

When a child is born, we know eighteen years later the child will be eighteen years old. However obvious this math is, many parents fail to put money away for college education.

My wife and I prayed to be blessed with children. Probably others do the same, and that is why I wonder why parents often ignore the cost of their children's education. Why wouldn't you put money aside for education and, in doing so, give your children an opportunity to compete in today's workforce? The answer may be that you don't know how, that you do not have the financial resources, or that you lack specific financial knowledge—even, that you don't see any real value in higher education.

Regardless of your reasons for not putting money aside for college, a 529 education plan may be just what you've been waiting for. A 529 plan is a tax-advantaged program designed to encourage saving for future higher-education expenses. Section 529 of the tax code defers taxes on your savings while you contribute and accumulate wealth inside the plan. When you withdraw the funds for education, the earnings are tax free. In states that impose an income tax, you may receive a credit or deduction for the amount invested each year. Check with your advisor.

I have invested in several tax-free mutual funds to generate monthly tax-free payments into our grandchildren's 529 plans. With that combination of investments, the tax-free monthly dividends are paid directly to the designated 529 plan, and I maintain total control over the amounts contributed and how the accounts are growing toward the appropriate amounts for college.

Generally, there are two people on each 529 account: the owner/custodian and the child/beneficiary of the program. There can be successor custodians, and should the original child be unable or unwilling to attend college, a successor beneficiary can be appointed. Substantial amounts, as defined by the individual state 529 plan, can be added to the account annually. The earnings in 529 plans, grow tax deferred, until the custodian requests withdrawals. If the proceeds are used for higher education, all the withdrawals are distributed tax-free, payable to the institution.

If the proceeds are not used for education, the withdrawal of earnings is considered taxable income to the owner/custodian and includes a 10% penalty. Some plans provide for non-education distributions to be pro-rated on a fifty-fifty basis at time of withdrawal, thereby reducing the taxable treatment to one half of the amount withdrawn. The taxable portion is treated as ordinary income with the addition of the 10% penalty.

Most 529 plans do not require that the beneficiary attend an institution in the state where the plan was created. In fact, the student may go wherever he or she wants. Another feature allows "late bloomers" to attend college as late as their thirties. Before you research the 529 market to determine which plan meets your objectives, make sure you encourage all family members to understand the importance of education.

College may not be for everyone, but did you know that according to the U.S. Census Bureau, a bachelor's degree can enable you to earn nearly twice as much as those with only a high-school diploma? Over a lifetime, a college graduate can earn $1 million more than someone without a degree. Is that enough incentive? The sacrifices you make today for a college education will pay off many times for your family in the future. And if you think education is expensive, consider the cost of ignorance!

"It's never too soon — start teaching them
about finances at an early stage in life."

18

Educate Children about Money

Everyone seems to be attracted to money.

In our family, we developed a system of discussing finances in a soft way, without making the subject boring or intimidating. We talked about different companies while sitting around our dinner table. Each Sunday, as we returned home from church, I took out the business section of the newspaper, laid it on the floor, and had our four children search for the stock of my employer. I asked for the closing price on Friday, the rate of dividends paid annually, and how much the stock price was up or down for the week. We then multiplied the closing price by the number of shares I owned in the company plan to determine the value of my account. As we arrived at the account balance, their eyes got big. To young kids, any amount parents had seemed like a lot.

We then searched the newspaper for other companies we were familiar with, such as McDonald's, Coca Cola, and General Electric. I asked them to tell me the closing price, whether it was up or down for the week, what dividends were paid, and how much the 100 shares we owned of each company would be worth. The kids looked forward to this exercise each week in order to demonstrate how smart they were. The competition among the four was fascinating. When we drove in to town to get a cheeseburger, I reminded the children that we owned part of this company. Sitting there in the car, they started to understand the opportunities for making money in our great country.

Most families treat financial education with the same uncomfortable feeling they might have treated sex education thirty years ago. Financial discussions continue to remain taboo because people, for the most part, do not understand this important subject. To make matters worse, most educators avoid teaching financial matters. Our country offers endless opportunities for accumulating wealth, and yet we don't teach anything about money in our schools. Why not? Think of your cost for a college education, and then ask your children, who are attending, how much they learned about the Number One subject in the world in those classes. You will be astounded at their response.

Staying current with stocks, bonds, mutual funds, annuities, and other investment vehicles in the market is vital to the financial health of our country.

It Gets Worse

Surveys tell us that the majority of kindergarten through twelfth grade teachers do not fully understand retirement planning and investing, and few fully participate in the 403(b) plans offered by their schools. If they don't understand how these retirement plans work, how can they convey the message of family financial planning and investing to their students? They don't!

With limited financial education, most Americans turn to news sources to learn about the markets. However, most newspaper and magazine journalists have little or no training in securities. They reside on the outside, looking in at the complicated world of investing. Without a securities license, these journalists can print whatever they like without regulatory repercussions, so readers get biased and often incorrect information—and they may use that information to make poor financial decisions. The problem becomes particularly worrisome when only one newspaper serves a metropolitan area. Biased reporting is further compounded by the absence of a veteran financial editor.

The result is that most readers are unfamiliar with the basics of family financial planning or investing. A simple, though unlikely, solution is for schools to offer classes in money management at all levels. By starting at an early age, students will become aware of the importance of maintaining a happy checkbook, investing, using credit cards properly, and managing debt. Then they will have a better chance of becoming financially successful as they grow into adulthood. Maybe some would become elected officials and, surprisingly, act in a responsible way with the resources of our great country. What a novel idea! The direction of our country could be changed forever.

INHERITED WEALTH

For many, inheriting wealth is a life-changing experience. Inheritance is instant wealth without the blood, sweat, and tears required to create it. There are so many sad stories of families who came unglued upon receiving an inheritance. Sometimes I think the beneficiaries should just say "no" to the new-found wealth. But they can't.

Parents who have devoted years to building a business or attaining a high income corporate career sometimes fail to devote an equal amount of time to their children. Highly successful parents are often completely consumed by their careers and, in their busyness, fail to discuss with their children how the business works. (The whole family needs to understand the family's business, personal income, and how to avoid abusing their level of success.)

For many, building a successful business or career requires nearly all their time and energy. Unfortunately, children of these parents are often kept out of the business and, therefore, never learn budgeting, business planning, or general wealth-building concepts. When these parents leave the firm, sell out, or die, the children are often overwhelmed with vast sums of money, yet have little knowledge of how to handle it.

These children, often at adult ages, want to know two things: how much there is and how quickly they can get it. This is after the parents' lifetime of managing the money to best maintain a secure retirement. Why are children of wealthy parents so matter-of-fact about their deceased parents' assets? I believe it's because they didn't work for the assets. Without the effort, children of wealthy parents have no emotional ties to the money.

An inheritance is similar to winning the lottery. Have you ever heard anyone say how much they appreciate winning the lottery? Initially, maybe. But after months of spending on frivolous purchases that bring little or no joy, with friends and family constantly asking for loans or demanding outright gifts, the winner loses appreciation for the windfall. I believe that deep down, most lottery winners and beneficiaries of large inheritances feel they don't deserve the money, and that's why they often squander it.

Another sad result of inheriting substantial wealth is that the parents have deprived their children of the desire to accomplish something important in life by creating their own legacy. These children lack ambition for financial achievements and successes because the money is already theirs. Creative talents and aspirations for individual recognition are lost forever. Inheriting substantial wealth can have negative psychological affects, as well. Some children think they are instantly experienced enough to handle the inheritance, and they often make poor decisions without proper guidance or expertise.

Learn to Respect Money

How can you, as a parent, handle these important matters for the family? Start to think like the wealthy and include a good advisor to manage your money. Introduce the advisor to your children to see if the relationship will continue to work in future years. This new relationship will reinforce the very same concepts that helped build the investment portfolio.

Ask your advisor about restricted beneficiary accounts, which can control the amount and the time frame of withdrawals, thereby helping the heirs better manage their inheritance in the event of a divorce or premature death in the family. Tell them how much you appreciate what your saving and investing have allowed you to accomplish. Let them know that your visible assets—homes, cars, and other purchases—are the outward expression of a solid foundation of diversified family holdings.

Teach your children early to appreciate saving as much as spending. This mindset can help create long-term family financial wealth and security for their families. Watch their eyes get big as you inject excitement into the discussion about family wealth.

You can make the goal of financial security a family tradition just like celebrating special holiday events. It should be openly discussed as a basic foundation to be passed to the next generations. Consider the confidence of family members as they realize they are all building wealth and status in life.

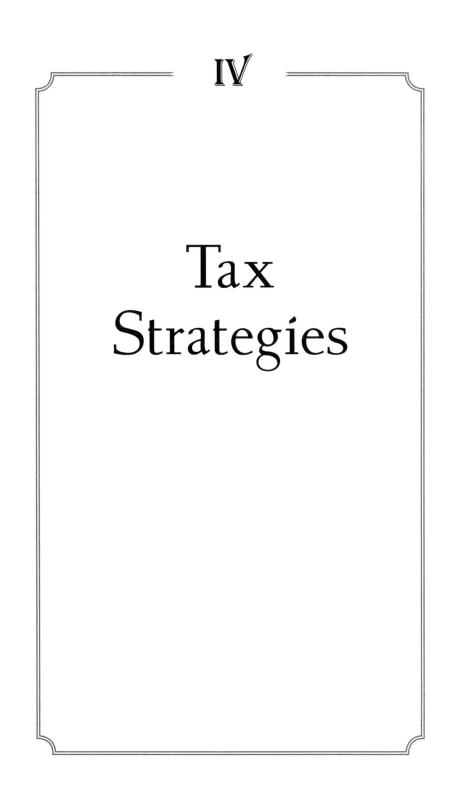

IV

Tax
Strategies

19

Know How to
Save Taxes

If we watched tax law or sausage
being made, we wouldn't accept either
one of them.

Many savers and investors are paying too much income tax each year. Are you one of them?

I am referring to most Americans who pay tax on money they aren't using. For example, think of the taxes you pay each year by having money in non-IRA mutual funds, or savings vehicles such as CDs, passbook savings, credit unions, and money market accounts, when you have no intention of withdrawing the funds until you retire. When you place your hard-earned family money in these programs, you must pay tax based on the 1099 earnings each year.

Why would you annually share your gains with the IRS and, in doing so, reduce your future retirement income? The taxes on capital gains and dividends are paid out of your pocket, so it is important to balance the amount you have in these various vehicles with your personal need for them. Check your tax return to determine what Form 1099s you receive each year and then discuss what changes can be made with your advisor.

Also, remember that CDs have surrender charges that

never go away. You may point out that the surrender charge is gone when the CD matures, but when it matures it is no longer a CD. It's time to change your way of thinking. Consider putting long-term money you presently have in CDs, credit unions, and money market accounts into tax-deferred or tax-free programs that allow you to save taxes and help reduce your annual tax filing paperwork. Depending on the choice of investment, earnings may be allowed to compound tax-free forever or tax-deferred until you withdraw the funds during retirement. That's a winning idea

The Dreaded IRS Form 1099

Each year in January, by law, financial institutions are required to mail a Form 1099, which reports various types of income other than wages, salaries, and tips. Generally, the 1099 is used to report interest, dividends, sales proceeds, and miscellaneous income.

Here is the problem: someone in the family is held responsible for receiving the envelope with Form 1099 inside. This person has to file the Form 1099 so it can be retrieved at tax time to calculate taxes. The more accounts you have, the more 1099s you receive. Receiving 1099s is a mess you won't have to deal with if you use tax-deferred instruments. There are no 1099s from these programs unless you withdraw income from your investments. This is one good way to simplify life as we get older.

If you are receiving Social Security benefits, the 1099 may affect their taxability. Discuss the tax consequences with your advisor to understand how certain programs could help you control taxes and reduce annual reporting requirements.

"You can pay me now."

20

Capital Gains Tax

Taxes are a problem only for those with money.

A capital gain is profit realized from the sale of an asset that has appreciated above its purchase price. For instance, stocks and bonds sold after being held for a certain period, as provided by our tax code, are taxed at a capital gains rate. The good news is that you made a gain on your investment; the bad news is that the gain is taxable. If you lost money on a venture, the loss is considered a capital loss and may be used to offset other gains dollar for dollar.

There are ways to delay paying capital gains taxes. Depending on the type of asset that created the gain, you may be able to defer the taxes. If you participate in a qualified plan such as a 401(k), 403(b), 457, pension plan, thrift plan, IRA, or a nonqualified variable annuity, all taxes on capital gains are deferred until you begin withdrawing the funds, which are then treated as ordinary income.

Tax-savvy folks will tell you, "Never accelerate the payment of taxes." This means you don't pay taxes until they are due. Consider the person who gets all the tax information together in January and realizes he or she owes taxes. The smart move is to hold the money as long as you can and pay your taxes no earlier than April 15. This delay gives you the use of the money for three more months to earn interest or to use as you see fit. Conversely, if you are getting a refund of overpaid taxes, file the tax return early. That's how smart money works!

Epilogue

As you come to the end of this book, I hope you realize that small, incremental changes in your financial habits can make huge improvements in your financial future. Now is the time to develop a whole new way to think about money, debt, savings, and investments. Basically, this new mindset is about forming new money habits that will become part of your family financial plan.

Although you may occasionally procrastinate or fall back into old habits, resist temptation and continue making positive steps each day. Celebrate small achievements and, in doing so, reinforce the concepts for all concerned. The past is the past. To be successful, you have to move up to the next level of financial maturity. Then you can expect positive results for the rest of your life.

You can do it. I know you can.

A 17-Point Plan
for Success

1. If you don't have the experience, time, or commitment to research the financial markets for investment information, develop a long-term relationship with a trusted financial advisor.

2. Decide on a goal. What is your working asset target number for retirement? Is it five hundred thousand, a million, ten million, or a whopping one hundred million? It's your life and your number—there are no limits!

3. Create a written family financial plan. If this sounds like too much effort, consider the following sample plan. Goal: to accumulate a certain amount in working assets that produce monthly income at the rate of 5% annually. That amount, combined with your Social Security benefits annually, produces the income to define your life style.

4. Pay off credit card debt each month and live beneath your means.

5. Learn the fundamental difference between savings and investments. Understand that long-term rate of returns for savings and investing can differ significantly.

6. Know the two enemies of money—inflation and taxes—and what to do about them.

7. Defer or eliminate taxes whenever possible by investing in tax-deferred or tax-free investments.

8. Invest the maximum allowed in your employer's retirement plan. Contact the proper department to obtain the forms, and complete them as soon as possible. Commit to understanding the plan, the special tax benefits, and how much you can contribute each pay period.

9. Start a monthly investment plan in a properly diversified growth and income program. One good approach is dollar-cost-averaging, a method of investing a set amount each month through payroll deductions or other means.

10. Consider the new guaranteed-income programs known as annuity living benefits.

11. If you have children, or grandchildren, invest in a tax-advantaged 529 education plan.

12. Always invest in programs that can produce monthly income. Consider ones that offer systematic monthly withdrawals high enough to live on without depleting your investments.

13. Have realistic expectations about the future performance of your investments.

14. Avoid anything, including rental homes, that you have to feed on a regular basis.

15. Remember that things that glitter are not investments. Direct your money into income-generating working assets.

16. Review your savings and investment account balances monthly to measure your asset growth progress.

17. Begin investing for your financial future today. Procrastination kills productivity.

NOTES

Amadoe, Kimberly, "Credit Card Debt Up 7.6%," About.com, May 9, 2007, http://useconomy.about.com/b/a/000056.htm.

Associated Press, "U.S. Gambling Revenues Up 6.8 Percent," *International Business Times*, May 8, 2007, http://www.ibtimes.com/articles/20070508/casino-industry.htm.

Bells, Mary, "Automobile History," About.com, July 2007, http://inventors.about.com/library/inventors/blcar.htm#history.

Federal Trade Commission, "Facts for Consumers, Buying a New Car," April 2006, http://www.ftc.gov/bcp/edu/pubs/consumer/autos/aut11.shtm.

FINRA, "We Are FINRA—The Financial Industry Regulatory Authority," July 2007, http://www.finra.org/index.htm.

Hall, Ed, U.S. National Debt Clock, http://www.brillig.com/debt_clock/ (accessed July 19, 2007).

The Humane Farming Association, "Texas Emu Rescue," July 2007, http://www.hfa.org/refuge/texas_emu.html.

Pearson Education, Inc., "Consumer Credit Outstanding and Finance Rates 1980 to 2000," Infoplease, http://www.infoplease.com/ipa/A0901305.html.

Sainz, Adrian, "Indian Gambling Revenues Up In 2006, But Growth Slows," *North Country Times*, June 28, 2007, http://www.nctimes.com/articles/2007/06/29/news/state/ 9_01_126_28_07.txt.

Stein, Robin, "The Ascendancy of the Credit Card Industry," Frontline, November 23, 2004, http://www.pbs.org/wgbh/pages/frontline/shows/credit/more/rise.html.

U.S. Department of Energy, "Average Price of a New Car 1970-2005 (Table 10.10)," *Transportation Energy Data Book*, http://www-cta.ornl.gov/data/tedb26/Spreadsheets/Table10_10.xls.

Wright, Richard A., "A Brief History of the First 100 Years of the Automobile Industry in the United States," The Auto Channel, 1996, http://www.theautochannel.com/mania/industry.orig/history/chap11.html.